Live Your
BEST CHAPTER

Napoleon Hill (1883–1970), best known for his global bestseller *Think and Grow Rich*, was a self-help author and businessman whose work has influenced millions across the world, from Norman Vincent Peale to Donald Trump. Born poor, Hill lived a colourful life, pursuing several different business ventures and professions. He also met and advised many famous people, such as US President Woodrow Wilson. Hill eventually found widespread success as a motivational author, writing several books on how to achieve success and practically creating the self-help genre.

Live Your

BEST CHAPTER

*Embrace **Achievement** and **Fulfillment***

NAPOLEON HILL

Published by
Rupa Publications India Pvt. Ltd 2024
7/16, Ansari Road, Daryaganj
New Delhi 110002

Sales centres:
Bengaluru Chennai
Hyderabad Jaipur Kathmandu
Kolkata Mumbai Prayagraj

Edition copyright © Rupa Publications India Pvt. Ltd 2024

All rights reserved.
No part of this publication may be reproduced, transmitted,
or stored in a retrieval system, in any form or by any means,
electronic, mechanical, photocopying, recording or otherwise,
without the prior permission of the publisher.

P-ISBN: 978-93-5702-844-8
E-ISBN: 978-93-5702-644-4

First impression 2024

10 9 8 7 6 5 4 3 2 1

Printed in India

This book is sold subject to the condition that it shall not, by way of
trade or otherwise, be lent, resold, hired out, or otherwise circulated,
without the publisher's prior consent, in any form of binding or
cover other than that in which it is published.

CONTENTS

1. The Basic Mental Attitude That Brings Wealth and Peace of Mind ... 7
2. It Is up to You to Live the Life the Creator Gave You ... 22
3. Enthusiasm ... 38
4. Co-operation ... 51
5. Inspire Teamwork ... 61
6. How to Motivate Yourself ... 70
7. Self-Confidence ... 78
8. The Golden Rule ... 100

1

THE BASIC MENTAL ATTITUDE THAT BRINGS WEALTH AND PEACE OF MIND

> A life of wealth enjoyed by a mind at peace comes most often to men who maintain a positive mental attitude. With definiteness of purpose, you add great positive power to your own mental attitude, and you can use definite motives to sustain the actions which propel you toward your goal. At the same time you can set up spiritual guardians to keep your attitudes at a high 'Yes' level, avoid conflicts of motive, tune-in on other positive minds.

The computers which are beginning to manage our world are complicated devices. Most of them, however, have a very simple basic principle: they say Yes or No. They either open a kind of electrical gate or they keep it closed, and by multiplying this process they can assimilate and select all kinds of information.

The mind of man is far more wonderful than any machine. Within it, however, there seems to be a kind of Yes-No valve at the focal point of thinking. It is as though your awareness of a circumstance of life—sent to your brain by your sight, hearing and other senses—presents itself at the Yes-No point to be processed. A person who maintains a positive attitude will find every possible Yes in that circumstance and make it part of his life. A person who maintains a negative mental attitude will lean toward the No side, miss much that is good, live with much that is painful and damaging.

Nothing but a mental attitude? Nothing but a mental attitude, but it is right there that your success or your failure, your peace of mind or your nervous tension, your tendency toward good health or your tendency toward illness begins.

Fortunately, it is possible for anyone to make the change from negativism to positivism, and thus basically condition his brain to bring all that is good in life. Moreover, there are certain 'control levers' which the Creator makes available to us, and it is easy to see how successful people use these levers, once you know what they are.

I shall give you some here and some in other chapters so as to reinforce your memory. Now and then you will find repetition of names, facts and methods in this book, always with a view toward helping you remember.

Control your mental attitude with definiteness of purpose. Emerson said, 'The world makes way for a man who knows where he is going.'

Think what it means to know where you are going! Automatically you rid yourself of all kinds of fears and doubts which may have crept into the making-up-your-mind process. Your purpose is definite and—presto!—all the limitless forces of your mind focus upon that purpose and no other. Knowing your purpose, you cannot be led astray by circumstances or words which have nothing to do with your purpose. Where, before, a day's work may have contained a good deal of wasted motion, now your efforts are lined up so that each mental or physical motion helps every other motion.

You can see the connection with building wealth, for work done well is a basic wealth-builder. Now see the connection with peace of mind. A man who works wholeheartedly at his job is not concerned with such matters as finding fault with others, disturbing his conscience by cutting corners in his work, watching the clock and so forth. Nor will he be discouraged by any obstacles which may crop up; his positive and focused mental attitude keeps him in a prime position to handle problems and overcome them.

EFFICIENCY AND POSITIVITY

Is this a secret of 'genius'? I have mentioned that many eminently successful men do not possess any greater intelligence than most other men possess. Yet their achievements are such that we may say that these men have 'genius'. Surely it is the positive mental attitude of these men which makes their brainpower, not greater, but more efficient and more available than most others. When I spoke to such men as Henry Ford, Andrew Carnegie and Thomas A. Edison, I spoke with minds free of any fear or doubt that they could do anything they wished to do.

I know that Andrew Carnegie was well aware of the need for a positive mental attitude. Before he undertook to back me in my success, he really put me 'on the spot' as to my mental attitude.

Looking at me shrewdly across his desk, that canny Scot said, 'We've talked a long time and I have shown you the greatest opportunity a young man ever had to become famous, rich and useful. Now—if I choose you out of the two hundred and forty other applicants for this job—if I introduce you to the outstandingly successful men in America—if I help you get their collaboration in finding out the true philosophy of success—will you devote twenty years to the job, earning your own living as you go along? We have had sufficient discussion. I want your answer—yes or no.'

I began to think of all the obstacles that would stand in my way. I began to think of all the hurdles I would have to jump. I began to think of all the time I would have to spend, and the big job of writing, and the problem of earning my living all that while—and so forth.

I spent twenty-nine seconds struggling with a negative mental attitude which, had it overcome me, would have affected me negatively ever after.

How do I know I took just twenty-nine seconds? Because, when I found the positive mental attitude which I had lost temporarily, and said, 'Yes!'—Mr Carnegie showed me the stopwatch he had been holding beneath his desk. He had given me just one minute in which to show my positive state of mind otherwise, he felt, he would not have been able to depend on it. I had beaten the deadline by just thirty-one seconds, and thereby embraced an opportunity that was destined to change and improve the lives of millions of people, including my own.

A positive mind tunes in on other positive minds. Once I had accepted that great task and had set my mind confidently toward it, I found that my imagined obstacles simply melted away. Of course, my positive mental attitude helped me not only in finding out the success secrets of some five hundred of America's wealthiest men, but also in making considerably more than a mere living. Am I a genius? I must say I have positive evidence I am not!

In meeting many men I discovered a very valuable fact: a positive mind automatically obtains benefit from other positive minds.

Are you aware of the general principle of radio broadcasting? It is this: when electrical vibrations of rapid frequency are impressed upon a wire, those vibrations leap into space. Another wire far away—the receiving antenna—can pick them up, and thus a message or a picture is transmitted over thousands of miles, or millions of miles in space-age communication.

There are electrical currents in the brain. They give you a private broadcasting station through which you may send out any kind of thought vibrations you desire. Keep that station busy sending out thoughts of a positive nature, thoughts which will benefit others, and you will find you can receive kindred thought vibrations from other minds whose attitude is tuned to yours.

When I visited such successful men as those I have mentioned, and many others such as John Wanamaker, Frank A. Vanderlip, Edward Bok and Woodrow Wilson, both they and I felt the attunement of mind to mind. Otherwise I surely would have met with opposition when I asked those top-ranking men to give me of their time and experience. Not only did such men spend hours talking to me, but also they served as my teachers and guides for year after year, and charged me nothing.

Believe in what you are doing, and you too will see the great effect of your belief upon those whom you may request to help you. Doubt yourself and the 'No' part of your mind takes over and draws defeat instead of victory.

This barely sketches in the all-pervasive power of a positive mental attitude. Let us look at some of the other 'control levers' which combine with a positive mental attitude to give you wealth and peace of mind for an entire, victorious lifetime.

THE NINE MAJOR MOTIVES

It is not for nothing that court trials often concern themselves with questions of motive. Everything you do is the result of one or more motives. In various combinations we use nine basic motives. The seven positive motives are:

1. The emotion of LOVE
2. The emotion of SEX
3. The desire for MATERIAL GAIN
4. The desire for SELF-PRESERVATION
5. The desire for FREEDOM OF BODY AND MIND
6. The desire for SELF-EXPRESSION
7. The desire for PERPETUATION OF LIFE AFTER DEATH

The two negative emotions are:

1. The emotion of ANGER AND REVENGE
2. The emotion of FEAR

In these nine motives you can find the roots of everything you do or refrain from doing. Peace of mind is attained only by the exercise of the seven positive motives as a general pattern of life. Rarely, if ever, does a person who has peace of mind exercise the two negative motives or emotions. You cannot have peace of mind while you fear anything or anyone. You cannot have peace of mind while you entertain the kind of anger which brings you to a desire for revenge or a desire to injure another, no matter what the justification may seem to be.

THE PRICE OF PEACE OF MIND

Great men have no time to waste with a desire to injure others. If they did, they would not be great men. Great men are not immune to fear, but theirs is not the kind of fear that hangs on constantly and takes over all of life. Look to small, mean men to see lifelong patterns of fear and anger. Their minds are so filled with these negative influences that they cannot find the power to shape the circumstances they desire.

Recently I heard about a man, now seventy, who fifteen years ago lost all his money in a real estate venture. Taking the advice of a friend, he had borrowed heavily in order to invest in vacant swampland on the assumption that in a couple of years the land would be in great demand for building lots. This did not transpire, the man's notes became due and he had to see his retail shoe business sold out from under him.

The friend who had badly advised him also had lost money. Nevertheless this man became filled with hatred toward his friend and said he would get even 'if it's the last thing I do.' It nearly was. Five years of hatred left him incapable even of doing business. Meanwhile the friend prospered and seemed far out of reach of any puny revenge. The man who had lost his money at length lost the balance wheel of his mind and had to spend six months in a quiet place in the country surrounded by a high wall.

In his last month of confinement, however, he was sufficiently recovered to listen to an adviser who pointed out to him that hatred and the desire for revenge had done him far more harm than had been done by his losing his money. He was persuaded to forgive the friend who had led him into the real estate deal. He even wrote to this man, telling of his change of heart.

When he went back into business it was with love of his

fellow men and the determination to keep his mind filled with positive, constructive motives. Beginning at the age of sixty, he built a new career. Now, at seventy, he is fairly well off, and most of all he has peace of mind, the one form of wealth which is indispensable.

I myself have suffered from the effects of negative motives from time to time. When I went into hiding, I acted at first upon a very wise motive of self-preservation. Soon, however, this turned into fear and with the fear came misery. Fortunately, I saw in time what was happening to me. It cannot happen again.

You can call upon Ten Princes of Guidance to stand at the doors of your mind. You can make yourself aware of certain principles of personal guidance and guardianship; and to make these principles real and memorable, you can personalize them—see them as so many Princes in armor who stand at the doors of your mind. These Princes challenge every thought-vibration which seeks to enter. They keep your mind positive, effective and free of discord. I shall name my own Princes, a list which you may wish to modify to suit your own life-requirements.

The Prince of Peace of Mind. He stands at the very outer door and asks all callers if they come in peace to share my peace. If not, they are turned away.

The Prince of Hope and Faith. He admits only those influences which keep my mind alerted with belief in my mission in life.

The Prince of Love and Romance. He brings into my mind only those influences which keep love eternally fresh in my heart.

The Prince of Sound Physical Health. He knows the kind of mental influences which can destroy health, and admits only those states of mind which help the body maintain its vigour.

The Prince of Financial Security. When I desire him to stand on guard, he admits no thoughts save those which bring me worthy financial benefit.

The Prince of Overall Wisdom. He is charged with passing certain thoughts into my store of knowledge when he sees they will benefit me or help me benefit others.

The Prince of Patience. He keeps away all impulses to rush, to tackle jobs half-prepared, to be in any way impatient with the power of time.

The Prince of Normhill. 'Normhill' is a very personal word I have created for my own use. Combining certain names, it means to me what it cannot mean to any other. Just so, create your own name for your own very personal Prince. This Prince stands guard along with all the others. The others from time to time may be relieved of duty; for instance, one hardly may wish continually to keep out all thoughts except those which have to do with financial security. Your special personal Prince is always there, representing all the special personal influences in your life. Normhill is my ambassador-at-large who performs services not assigned to the other members of my invisible family of guides.

When you have made yourself well aware of your corps of spiritual Princes, they serve to rally all your forces to solve any problem or to set up special lines of defence.

Sometimes I find myself talking to someone whose antagonistic attitude begins to invade my peace of mind. Very well—I send a special alert to the Prince of Peace of Mind. Immediately he takes charge of the ramparts with doubled strength, and I am calm and in control of my own mind once more.

Or, let us say, I feel some physical ache or pain. I call upon the Prince of Sound Physical Health to look into the cause, and I get good results. I believe I have received benefits of healing which are beyond the power of ordinary medical science to explain.

My Princes of Guidance receive a certain compensation for their services. Their 'pay' is my eternal gratitude. Daily I express this gratitude, first to each of the Princes individually, then to all of them in their mighty group. You will find this expression of gratitude of great help in keeping your mind alerted to its own powers. I know that if I ever neglect it, I feel a neglect on the part of my Princes. When, once again, I make myself aware every day that I have great spiritual forces at my command—there they are once more, as strong as ever.

Don't let the motive of material gain conflict with the motive of freedom. Freedom of body is easy to see and understand; but freedom of mind is a subtle matter. Fear and anger put the mind behind bars. Guilt wraps the mind in chains. To add a bit of levity to a serious matter: once there was a man who was encouraged to know himself. Immediately he handcuffed himself to his bed, so he would not get up and rifle his own pockets during the night.

All too often the motive of material gain—excellent in itself—conflicts with the excellent motive of freedom of body and mind because in gaining what is material we give up freedom of mind; we load the mind with guilt and fear because we do not act honestly.

In addition, one who makes his money through taking dishonest advantage of his fellow men has cheated himself of the genuine joy which comes with honest success. When you obey the rules of a game, and win, you have done something for your soul. When you cheat and win, you only call it winning, but you have really lost instead.

I believe I was fortunate in starting my career very early

in life, so that I learned life's lessons quite early. Let me tell you of an experience I had while I was holding my first job. I was just out of business college and I was inexperienced in the ways of life and the character of men.

My employer owned a number of banks. He had placed his son as a cashier of one of his banks, in a distant town. One night a hotel manager in that town telephoned me, saying my employer's son was in serious difficulty. He had not been able to reach my employer. Immediately, I boarded the train and arrived in the town early the next morning.

When I went to the bank I found the door closed but unlocked. Inside, I discovered that the vault had been left open and beautiful green currency was scattered all over the teller's counter.

I closed the door and picked up the telephone. I managed to get my employer on the phone and told him why I had gone to that town and what I had found on my arrival. In great distress, he said, 'Go ahead and count the money. Balance the books. Draw a draft on me for whatever shortage there may be.'

I settled down to counting the money. To my great surprise, not a cent was missing.

I sat there looking at those piles of greenbacks. My youth had been tragic, turbulent and poor. My present state was one of bare solvency. I sat there looking at nearly $50,000 in cash, knowing that I could put at least half of it into my pocket and nobody would be the wiser. My employer's son showed obvious signs of mental instability. Everyone would assume he had taken the money. He even had acted as though he had filled his own pockets—and I was the only one who knew he had not.

The motive of material gain nudged heavily at me. But the motive of freedom said: don 't do it. Or rather, it was 'something' that kept me honest, for at that time I could not have named the major motives. Perhaps that 'something' was the result of certain sessions I had had with my stepmother before I had left home, in which she had instilled into me the fact that I was in control of my own mind and that always I must live with myself.

I locked the money into the vault forthwith, then phoned my employer and told him there was no deficiency to make up; not a cent had been stolen. I walked out of that bank with a mind at peace, a mind that was free and joyously positive.

Forever after I have placed the motive of freedom ahead of the motive of material gain. I have succeeded in having all the money I need without ever hampering either my inward or outward freedom.

LIFE IS A MIRROR

This episode was one of several which led me straight to Andrew Carnegie and my realization of my goal in life. My employer was grateful for the way in which I had protected his son's reputation as best I could. He was responsible later for my entering Georgetown University Law School. This led through a chain of circumstances to my assignment to interview Mr Carnegie. If I had yielded to the material gain motive that day in the bank, the Science of Personal Achievement might never have come into being.

Yes, as Emerson suggested, there is a silent partner in all our transactions, and woe is the lot of the man who tries to drive a sharp bargain with Life.

Life reflects your own thoughts back to you. Thoughts are things, a poet said, and truly they have an existence of their own, so that a curse comes back to curse you and a blessing comes back to bless you, reflected by the mighty mirror of life.

Another poet said, 'I am the master of my fate, I am the captain of my soul.' This too is true, and the two truths harmonize. Send out positive thoughts from a positively oriented soul and the world will reflect back greater and greater positive influences to help you.

Turn back and read the list of nine basic motives. Concentrate on the seven positive motives. Remember it is possible for these motives to come into conflict, as we have seen; but by and large they drive one way, and with a positive mental attitude they take you the way you want to go. We shall not say farewell to the motives till we are finished with this book; but let us now pay our respects briefly.

Love has limitless scope. Handle it in a spirit of reverence, for it is tuned to the Eternal. Give freely of it and you will attract as much as or more than you give; stop giving love and you stop receiving. With no other emotion or motive or desire is the mirror of life so very evident.

Sex is the great creative force of the universe. On its highest plane it merges with love; but love can exist without being sexual. The mighty power of sex can be transmuted into action for the achievement of profound purpose. On the other hand, sex may be debauched and misused, and it is in this guise that it brings grief and trouble to mankind and gives itself an underserved bad reputation.

Self-preservation can become a negative force when one seeks it without regard to the rights of other people. It is instilled by Nature to help us stay alive. Even so, the human being assumes the prerogative of rising above it. When a ship is sinking it is *women and children first*, and there are many parallel instances which call forth a nobility in human nature.

Self-expression is part of finding one's self. It is part of one's freedom to be one's self. Thus it is positive, constructive and infinitely valuable. Only make sure that your own means of self-expression do not demean or damage others.

Perpetuation of life after death belongs among the earliest beliefs and motives of mankind. It should be bounded by common sense and a true understanding of one's relationship to that change known as death. When wrapped in superstition and fear, this motive leads only to wretchedness. It can turn life into a preparation for death and hamper an entire civilization.

The surest way of finding peace of mind. The surest way of finding peace of mind is that which helps the greatest number of others to find it.

Let this be your guide to your use of the great motivating forces; then you will know you are using them correctly, not corrupting them.

Is there peace of mind in prayer? There can be. There *should* be. But note how many people go to prayer only in the hour of a misfortune, when the motive of fear dominates their minds. The approach must be negative in that case, and so, in terms of peace of mind, the results must be negative as well.

Prayers which bring peace of mind proceed from a mind which gives forth a confident message even though that mind may be afflicted with problems and sorrow. Prayers which free great forces to solve problems are born in minds which know that the problems can be solved once the forces are found—and have perfect confidence in the existence of those forces.

Along with many others I see evidence of an Intelligence beyond man's. I believe that the positively conditioned mind may at times tune in on that Intelligence. Yet mind-conditioning through prayer or resolution is something an individual must accomplish for himself. When the Creator made man free to seek his own destiny, and choose between good and evil, he gave man this prerogative as well. Every great accomplishment of any man at any time first had to exist as a thought before it could exist as reality.

Have you recognized the Supreme Secret?

POINTS TO REMEMBER

1. A life of wealth is only enjoyed by someone who possess a positive mental attitude.
2. Control your mental attitude with definiteness of purpose.
3. The nine basic motives for any human endeavour.

2

IT IS UP TO YOU TO LIVE THE LIFE THE CREATOR GAVE YOU

The Golden Rule can be applied all-out in a way that will transform our economy for the better. When people are helped to turn their ideas into the realities of business and production, everyone in the United States will have more wealth and happiness. Most of us believe in man-made gods and man-made devils. Fear has no place in a well-lived life. Put your faith, not in a Creator who bosses you but One who makes it possible for you, as a human being, to win success by your own efforts. Wealth now can be yours. Peace of mind now can be yours at the same time, but remember, this greatest of all wealth is known only to the person who possesses it.

'Help me find peace of mind,' the rich man said.

This was some years ago. A trip across the country was not then a matter of six hours in a jet plane, but he had come across the country to talk to me. 'I have everything money can buy,' he said, 'and I have lived long enough to find out that money cannot buy peace of mind. Please help me find it.'

A good part of this chapter consists of what we discussed,

and which I shall give to you in a conversational manner. First we went into everything this book has covered—I shall omit that part—and then we branched out into what has been for many years my most cherished project.

It is a business project—and a peace-of-mind project. It could bring joy and prosperity to millions of men and women, especially to those who need help in finding their places in life. It would work hand in hand with our American economy. It would not be a 'make work' project, since it would provide services whose need is proved. It would make profit—that indispensable factor whose virtues have at length been recognized even in the Soviet Union. It would be a business project that first of all would be a human project devoted to creating wealth through sharing wealth.

A job for a dedicated man. 'Before I tell you about my project,' I said to my visitor, 'I want to make it clear that it will need a dedicated man to get it going. A man who has plenty of money, plenty of time, and plenty of executive know-how, for all these are needed to turn the idea into reality. He would have to be a man who would go to work with no thought of what *he* would get out of his efforts. I say he would have to have plenty of money because he might lose some of his money—and he would also have to be psychologically suited to accept this fact without losing the peace of mind the project would give him.'

'Tell me more,' said the man from California.

'Well then, what I have in mind is a nationwide organization to be called The Golden Rule Industries of America.'

The visitor looked puzzled. 'Where does the Golden Rule come in?'

'Suppose you had just about enough money to live on, or even less, but you had a sound business idea you wanted to develop. What would you like someone to do unto you?'

'I surely would like someone to come along and give me capital!'

'That's what I meant. The Golden Rule Industries of America would devote itself to finding people who have sound business ideas, capitalizing those ideas and helping those people get started in their businesses. Then it would follow up with business management advice, as might be necessary. It would take care of the two major factors which make businesses fail—lack of capital and unsound management. It would fill those needs for honest people who want to get ahead but cannot fill those needs for themselves.'

My visitor looked thoughtful. 'There must be thousands of such cases.'

'I am sure there are. Let me tell you of a few I know to exist.

'There is a young woman who is clever at designing. She wants to design and manufacture women's garments for the retail trade. Golden Rule Industries could set her up in business, make sure she got started on the right foot, and watch her grow. Eventually she would give employment to hundreds of people. Bear in mind that she, and every other person whom Golden Rule Industries aids with capital and business advice, will be a person who applies the Golden Rule to others, employees in particular. Golden Rule means that too.' 'I see.'

'A mechanic has built a model of an automobile which can be manufactured and sold for one thousand dollars. It will travel fifty miles to the gallon, will carry three people—ideal for the small family—and is so simple of design that its upkeep will be very small. Golden Rule Industries could set up this man in a small shop and let him expand as his business justifies. Undoubtedly the entire automobile industry would respond with better cars at lower prices.

'A bright high school boy builds excellent model airplanes. He wants to develop his skill into a national business and employ other high school boys, after school, as his staff. Golden Rule Industries could help this youth and his friends start a business and develop it.'

'That would be a wonderful head start toward a productive life!' my visitor exclaimed.

'It certainly would. I have in mind, too, a certain poor farmer. I have sympathy with poor farmers. This man wants to introduce the growing of a certain fibre plant now being developed in Africa, which can be grown in our southern states. There is an undoubted future in this, and Golden Rule Industries could provide this man with the land, machines and employees he needs.

'A young author has written a very creditable novel based on life in the mountains of Tennessee. He has not been able to get it published, but Golden Rule Industries could take it over for him and capitalize its publication if need be.

'A young lady stenographer has invented a chair so designed that it moves back and forth with the movement of the body and adjusts itself to fit the curvature of the back. This is a great idea. It will lessen fatigue, improve work and should have a tremendous market. It would be a real pay deal for Golden Rule Industries.'

'Where do these ideas come from?' my visitor wanted to know.

'Many of them represent cases I have handled for my clients. In my endeavours to help people stand on their own feet, I became aware of the many who have good ideas and plenty of ability, and need only capital and good management advice in order to get started. Now let me tell you of a rather special area in which Golden Rule Industries could do a world of good.

'In every prison there are many well-educated men capable of conducting business and educational courses for the benefit of the other inmates. This could result in these men being ready, willing and able to lead honest, useful lives when they are freed. A group of businessmen tried out this plan in the Ohio State Penitentiary, and it worked like a charm. The International Correspondence Schools contributed more than thirty-five thousand dollars' worth of textbooks. The plan could be expanded greatly—and it is society that would profit. I have personally appropriated this idea and it is creating miracles of rehabilitation in many prisons.

'A mechanic has made a model of a prefabricated dwelling made of aluminium sections. Any able man with a couple of helpers can set up the walls and roof in a day's time and start living in the house with his family while he finishes the interior. There are similar houses on the market, but this one also can be taken down as easily as it is put up, and moved to another location, without damage to its components.'

'There's profit in that idea,' said the man from California.

'Yes, and I have a number of other ideas just as profitable. Many of them need only some way to get started despite the opposition of established interests who see only that their business world be affected, without seeing the benefit to the economy at large. Now let us digress from the business ideas themselves and look at Golden Rule Industries' general policy.

'Golden Rule Industries should be developed with the idea that it will pay a profit in itself as it goes along. I would, therefore, incorporate the idea of profit-sharing. Each enterprise would pay back to the Industries 10 per cent of its net earnings. Half of this amount would go to the Industries for the use of the capital and the business management. The other 5 per cent would be used as a payment on the original investment.

When the investment was fully repaid, each enterprise would pay the Industries 5 per cent of its net earnings thereafter in return for management services and other services which might be necessary.

'You can see that this policy would create a revolving fund which could be used over and over to help more and more enterprises get started. But no enterprise would be bound forever to the Industries. After it paid back its capitalization, it could leave the Industries. We wouldn't want a monopoly. But I am quite sure that even if an enterprise left the Industries, it would continue on the Golden Rule basis of sharing the wealth it creates with its own employees, for it would be apparent by then that this is the way to make a business and its people prosper.'

My visitor had arrived in my office with a woebegone face. Now he was vibrant and looked ten years younger. 'That's great!' he exclaimed. 'And I can see that one business after another would want to come in and join hands in such an undertaking. Why, it's the best way I ever heard of to prevent strikes and other labour troubles.'

'I believe it would create harmony and peace of mind where those qualities are badly needed,' I said. 'And it would create all-important self-respect in giving people an opportunity to help themselves instead of feeding at the public trough at the expense of others. The plan would have a sweeping effect on our entire economy.

'Moreover, The Golden Rule Industries of America should operate its own radio and TV station. There would be no commercials. All the broadcasting time would be devoted to teaching people, in their own homes, all the essentials of personal achievement. People would find out at last that success is an inward matter which each of us must build within himself, rather than waiting for someone to hand him what he needs. We will have a nation that does not look for "isms" to take care of it—a nation of people who will work hard to create wealth, in the happy confidence that they will receive a good share.'

'Great heavens, man!' my visitor broke in. 'You are talking about the millennium.'

'No,' I said, 'I am presenting a practical plan to save this nation from destruction by the greedy who have not yet learned the necessity—and the virtue—of sharing riches.

'Golden Rule Industries would go beyond the transformation of industry in improving this land of ours. It would run a school for training men and women for public office—everything from dog-catcher to President. I hope this school eventually would attain such status as to make sure the voters may select public servants on the basis of their ability—instead of on their astuteness in swinging votes with the application of suitable amounts of money.'

'Amen, amen!' said my visitor.

'Along with this school of political economy there would be a citizens' committee of men and women who are capable of examining and grading all candidates for public office. The people would once again come into full possession of their government.'

'Great! But don't you think there would be a great deal of opposition to your plan—both industry-wise and government-wise? After all, you shut out a lot of nice, juicy opportunities for exploitation.'

'I'd expect opposition,' I replied. 'Opposition is a healthy circumstance. It makes one either prove the soundness of his plan or discover its weaknesses. I'd expect to make adjustments as I went along.

'There are other features I have in mind for Golden Rule

Industries which might provoke even more opposition. The power of the Industries' centralized buying would be such as to cause howls from those who think only of profit. When we helped our members buy homes of their own—as I believe should be done—there'd be screams of socialism—from other interests.

'When we helped Industries' members, including their employees, with such services as may be given by physicians, dentists, attorneys, even beauticians—and made sure they received the finest service at the lowest possible fees—the screams would rise to a crescendo. In the end, however, it would be recognized that the plan represents democracy operating on the highest possible scale of efficiency. All men who wish to live and let live will welcome this plan that adds so much to living. Our strength would lie in the fact that such people vastly outnumber the people who want to dominate and exploit others.'

My visitor thought a moment. 'And this would begin with finding people who have sound business ideas, and getting them into action.'

'That is right. It would bring worthy beliefs of the human mind onto the plane of worthy achievement. The more we have in the world of this process, the better world we build.'

My visitor sat a while. At last he arose and laid some large bills on my desk.

'I want you to have this honorarium in return for the help you have given me. I am going to swing into action with a new and better philosophy of life than any I ever have known in the past. I do not know if I am the man with the money, the time, the philosophy and the business experience to initiate Golden Rule Industries. But I see now what life can be when men cooperate in the production of goods and services for each other. I see why I made money but never found peace of mind. I see what has been lacking in my life, and I feel better, Dr Hill. Yes, sir, I feel better than I have felt in years. You have done more for me than a number of doctors have been able to do.'

My visitor never returned. Golden Rule Industries still remains a dream yet, in part, it is a dream I see coming true. Our economy grows less and less the hunting ground of the industrial pirate. It is only here and there that I see the development of co-operation, but I do see that groundswell of sharing the wealth, and it is this philosophy, based on the Golden Rule, which will keep America great; not the practice of handing out government doles to people who have done nothing to deserve them.

ABSTAIN FROM MAN-MADE INFLUENCES

Peace of mind vs. man-made gods and man-made devils. You see by now that the power of firm, free belief comes with an untrammelled mind: the power to turn what the human mind believes into what the human mind achieves rarely can be found by a man who is hemmed in with fear and misdirection.

There are some exceptions. You can see men in business still making money while they harm others in making it, but this type is nowhere nearly as prevalent as it was fifty years ago.

You can see exceptions elsewhere, too. Unfortunately, the human mind is capable of believing in man-made images which it sets up as Great Truths. This belief can lead to so-called achievement on its own plane; for instance, the achievement of great societies known as religions which teach that you will fry in Hell if you do not believe certain things.

I write here for strong people—for people who realize that the most cherished beliefs nevertheless can be wrong in that they hinder the development of the human spirit. They claim to develop that spirit—but they develop it as much as a man's view of the world would be developed if he walked in a narrow alley between two high walls all his life.

Regardless of your emotions right now, surely you have been impressed by the fact that the Creator provided you with control over your own power of thought and made it impossible for any person to rob you of this privilege—unless you let him.

In my decades of research into the roots of personal achievement, I came across a book called Catalogue of the Gods. This book gave a brief description of each of the THIRTY THOUSAND man-made gods which men have worshiped since the beginning of civilization. Yes, THIRTY THOUSAND.

These sacred objects ranged all the way from the common angle-worm to the sun which warms our earth. They included almost every conceivable object between these two extremes, such as fish, snakes, tigers, cows, birds, rivers, oceans and the genital organs of man.

Who made these objects into gods? Man himself. Which ones were authentic gods? Ask any worshiper and he would tell you, and eventually you would have a list of thirty thousand authentic gods, one just as authentic as another.

If I undertook to describe the miseries of mankind which can be laid at the feet (if they had feet) of those thirty thousand gods, and the fears and miseries and failures they have inspired in the minds of men, I would need more than one lifetime in which to do the job properly.

Man made a great step forward in his own behalf when he began to see a Creator, not gods, and removed this Creator from any connection with earthly objects. The ancient Hebrews performed this service for man. (One of the Egyptian kings appears to have come to the same conclusion some centuries before they did, but his priests saw to it that he died young.)

Yet what have we done with this belief? My own case is the one I know best. Until my father married the woman who saved me, the family in which I grew up was dominated by fear. It contributed to the support of an organization dedicated to maintaining that fear; it is known as the Hard-shell Baptists.

A preacher could visit our community only once a month, but on those occasions I was forced to listen to four or five hours of preachment. We were thundered at with pictures of a Hell waiting to receive us with fire and brimstone, and at times I could smell the stuff burning.

One night when I was seven or eight, I dreamed I was down there chained to an iron post. My body was almost covered with a great pile of fresh brimstone. Here came Satan, swishing his tail and with an evil grin he set fire to the brimstone. I awoke screaming. One needs no formal knowledge of psychology to know this is not good for any child. But when I tried to stay away from the church that gave me dreadful nightmares, I was thrashed without mercy.

The Creator I know. One day I overheard my stepmother say to my father, 'The only real devil that exists in this or any other world is the man whose business is that of making devils.' I accepted this statement instantly and never have departed from it.

I have taken pains to put into this book the fact that my father's prayers seemed to have focused powers of healing beyond medicine, which saved my life when I had typhoid fever. That was his time of faith, not fear.

In denying that I have anything to fear, I also deny that anyone has knowledge enough to tell me anything definite about the spirit that rules the universe.

A theologian might say—although these days they are becoming wary of saying it, 'Somewhere up there is Heaven, where God dwells, and all His acceptable children go there when they leave their earthly bodies, and gather around Him.' A scientist might say, 'I have turned my telescope outward into space in all directions. I have looked into space for distances equivalent to millions of light-years, but nowhere do I see the slightest trace of anything resembling Heaven.'

The Creator whom I know is not separated from me by light-years nor by any other distance. I see evidence of His existence in every blade of grass, every flower, every tree, every creature on this earth, in the order of the stars and the plants which float out there in space, in the electrons and protons of matter and most especially in the marvellous working principles of the human mind and the body within which it operates.

If you would rather speak of a force or a presence for a limitless intelligence rather than a Creator, it is the same. It is there. Is it affected by our worship? I doubt it. Can we sometimes attune ourselves so that we receive help from universal vibrations? This, I believe, is almost certainly true.

THE FINAL TRUTH

I do not even attempt to guess the over-all purpose or plan behind the universe. So far as I can tell, there is no plan for man except to come into this world, live a little while, and go. While he lives, he is given the opportunity to make himself and his fellow men better beings, perhaps a more advanced form of man, as Lecomte du Noüy suggests. But—his ultimate purpose? I do not think anyone knows more about that than I know, and I know nothing about it.

Your greatness is here and now. Your happiness is here and now. Here are some of the factors which create peace of mind. They are involved in creating money-wealth as well; but let us set that aside for the time being. Here are some peace-of-mind factors; read them carefully; note that you have met them in this book, in one form or another, and *note that you have heard about them from other sources as well.*

You must come to realize you have a conscience which will guide you, and stay on good terms with your conscience so it will guide you well.

You must take possession of your own mind, do your own thinking, live your own life.

You must keep yourself so busy living your own life that you will not be tempted to interfere in the lives of others.

You must learn to free your life of unnecessary encumbrances, both material and mental.

You must establish harmony in your own home and harmony with those among whom you work.

You must share your blessings with others, and do this wholeheartedly.

You must look at the realities of life as they are, not as you wish them to be, and properly evaluate them.

You must help others to find and develop their own powers to make themselves what they want to be.

Now, I did not invent these ways of winning peace of mind. They were known of old. They are the ways which have proved themselves right, strong and eternal. If I have made these ways more clear to you, and if I have given you practical ways in which to apply them, well and good; but the wisdom behind them is the gathered wisdom of mankind.

And so you have heard before of these peace-of-mind factors. Perhaps they were told to you as ways to help yourself get to Heaven. This belief leaves you up against a blank wall. I give them to you as representative of the tried and true methods which help you live a healthier, wealthier, better life, here, on this earth, now. Is this not sufficient?

The Creator in your life. You have seen that I do not deny the concept of a Creator as an eternal and all-pervading intelligence, or cosmic force. But the Creator with whom I made my peace many years ago does not require me to be afraid of Him; nor does He offer Himself to me merely through the intervention of any particular religion.

My Creator gave me His greatest blessing when He made me human.

He gave me the power to choose between good and bad, and made my concept as wide as all the affairs of the world and all its people. He set me at large upon the world to learn that my good deeds are rewarded in kind, and my bad deeds are just as inexorably made to draw penalties according to their nature. He gave me a mind beyond the mind of any other of His creatures, and He made me free to use my mind as only a human being can use his mind-power.

I can pray, and in constructive prayer that does not amount to begging for special favours. I can find faith which vastly enlarges my powers. Yet always I know I am the master of my fate, I am the captain of my soul, for so my Creator made me, and so I need not call upon Him constantly for guidance. Have you ever noticed that the one who does the praying very often has a large part in the answering of the prayer? I allow for the prayer that goes Beyond; but I believe that many a prayer stays within the one who prays and strengthens him in his realization of his own human abilities.

The Creator's place in your life is to help you be more triumphantly your own master. The Creator made you a creature who can think for himself, be himself, believe in what he wishes to accomplish, and mightily achieve! Do less than this and you cannot possibly fulfil yourself in all your glorious humanity.

The mind of man is filled with powers to be used, not to be neglected. These powers, these blessings, either are used—and the benefits of their use shared with others—or you incur penalties for not using them.

If you needed a house, and knew how to build a house, and had all the materials you needed for building a house, and had a lot on which to build a house, and yet neglected to build a house—then you would understand your penalty as you sat exposed in the rain and the snow.

Too many of us do not use our power to gather in the wealth and peace of mind which is available all around us. Then we are penalized by poverty, by misery, by worry and ill health—and we blame everyone but ourselves.

Anything the human mind can believe, the human mind can achieve.

Believe in poverty and you will be poor.

Believe in wealth and you will be rich.

Believe in love and you will have love.

Believe in health and you will be healthy.

You have seen what lies behind these statements. It would be well to read this book again and refresh your understanding. No book can give you all its wealth at the first reading. Make friends with this book, read it again, put it away for a while, take it out and read it once more, and you will read much between the lines—and much that applies to you.

I have shared with you what may be merely words, or great

wealth and contentment—depending on how you use them. I am glad I cannot force you to use the knowledge I have given you. I am glad it is up to you to improve your own life.

I leave you now with no great ceremony.

Remember: there is no good thing in the world that is not available to you if you sufficiently desire it.

And remember: no matter what others may see of your possessions after you make a great deal of money…no matter how they may respect your offices and influence and talents… no matter how much they may admire your generosity, your kindliness, your willingness to live and let live…you yourself are the only one who can hold and enjoy your greatest treasure, peace of mind.

Cherish your visions and your dreams. They are the children of your soul, the blueprints of your ultimate achievements.

POINTS TO REMEMBER

1. Fear has no place in a well-lived life.
2. Peace of mind, the greatest of the riches and how to find it.
3. Find the power to turn what the human mind believes into what the human mind achieves.

3

ENTHUSIASM

Enthusiasm is a state of mind that inspires and arouses one to put *action* into the task at hand. It does more than this—it is contagious, and vitally affects not only the enthusiast, but all with whom he comes in contact.

Enthusiasm bears the same relationship to a human being that steam does to the locomotive—it is the vital moving force that impels *action.* The greatest leaders of men are those who know how to inspire enthusiasm in their followers. Enthusiasm is the most important factor entering into salesmanship. It is, by far, the most vital factor that enters into public speaking.

If you wish to understand the difference between a man who is enthusiastic and one who is not, compare Billy Sunday with the average man of his profession. The finest sermon ever delivered would fall upon deaf ears if it were not backed with enthusiasm by the speaker.

HOW ENTHUSIASM WILL AFFECT YOU

Mix enthusiasm with your work and it will not seem hard or monotonous. Enthusiasm will so energize your entire body that you can get along with less than half the usual amount of sleep and at the same time it will enable you to perform from two to three times as much work as you usually perform in a given period, without fatigue.

For many years I have done most of my writing at night. One night, while I was enthusiastically at work over my typewriter, I looked out of the window of my study, just across the square from the Metropolitan tower, in New York City, and saw what seemed to be the most peculiar reflection of the moon on the tower. It was of a silvery grey shade, such as I had never seen before. Upon closer inspection 1 found that the reflection was that of the early morning sun and not that of the moon. It was daylight! I had been at work all night, but 1 was so engrossed in my work that the night had passed as though it were but an hour. I worked at my task all that day and all the following night without stopping, except for a small amount of light food.

Two nights and one day without sleep, and with but little food, without the slightest evidence of fatigue, would not have been possible had I not kept my body energized with *enthusiasm* over the work at hand.

Enthusiasm is not merely a figure of speech; it is a vital force that you can harness and use with profit. Without it you would resemble an electric battery without electricity.

Enthusiasm is the vital force with which you recharge your body and develop a dynamic personality. Some people are blessed with natural *enthusiasm*, while others must acquire it. The procedure through which it may be developed is simple. It begins by the doing of the work or rendering of the service which one likes best. If you should be so situated that you cannot conveniently engage in the work which you like best, for the time being, then you can proceed along another line very effectively by adopting a *definite chief aim* that contemplates your engaging in that particular work at some future time.

Lack of capital and many other circumstances over which you have no immediate control may force you to engage in work which you do not like, but no one can stop you from determining in your own mind what your *definite chief aim* in life shall be, nor can anyone stop you from planning ways and means for translating this aim into reality, nor can anyone stop you from mixing *enthusiasm* with your plans.

Happiness, the final object of all human effort, is a state of mind that can be maintained only through the hope of future achievement. Happiness lies always in the future and never in the past. The happy person is the one who dreams of heights of achievement that are yet unattained. The home you intend to own, the money you intend to earn and place in the bank, the trip you intend to take when you can afford it, the Position in life you intend to fill when you have prepared yourself and the preparation, itself—these are the things that produce happiness. Likewise, these are the materials out of which your *definite chief aim* is formed; these are the things over which you may become *enthusiastic*, no matter what your present station in life may be.

More than twenty years ago I became enthusiastic over an idea. When the idea first took form in my mind I was unprepared to take even the first step toward its transformation into reality. But I nursed it in my mind—I became *enthusiastic* over it as I looked ahead, in my imagination, and saw the time when I would be prepared to make it a reality.

The idea was this: I wanted to become the editor of a magazine, based upon the Golden Rule, through which I could inspire people to keep up courage and deal with one another squarely.

Finally my chance came! and, on armistice day, 1918, I wrote the first editorial for what was to become the material realization of a hope that had lain dormant in my mind for nearly a score of years.

With *enthusiasm* I poured into that editorial the emotions which I had been developing in my heart over a period of more than twenty years. My dream had come true. My editorship of a national magazine had become a reality.

As I have stated, this editorial was written with *enthusiasm*. I took it to a man of my acquaintance and with *enthusiasm* I read it to him. The editorial ended in these words, 'At last my twenty-year-old dream is about to come true. It takes money, and a lot of it, to publish a national magazine, and I haven't the slightest idea where I am going to get this essential factor, but this is worrying me not at all because *I know 1 am going to get it somewhere!*' As I wrote those lines, I mixed *enthusiasm* and faith with them.

I had hardly finished reading this editorial when the man to whom I read it—the first and only person to whom I had shown it—said, 'I can tell you where you are going to get the money, for I am going to supply it.' And he did!

Yes, *enthusiasm* is a vital force; so vital, in fact, that no man who has it highly developed can begin even to approximate his power of achievement.

Before passing to the next step in this lesson, I wish to repeat and to emphasize the fact that you may develop *enthusiasm* over your *definite chief aim* in life, no matter whether you are in position to achieve that purpose at this time or not. You may be a long way from realization of your *definite chief aim*, but if you will kindle the fire of *enthusiasm* in your heart, and keep it burning, before very long the obstacles that now stand in the way of your attainment of that purpose will melt away as if by the force of magic, and you will find yourself in possession of power that you did not know you possessed.

HOW YOUR ENTHUSIASM WILL AFFECT OTHERS

We come, now, to the discussion of one of the most important subjects of this Reading Course, namely, *suggestion*.

Suggestion is the principle through which your words and your acts and even *your state of mind* influence others. If you now understand and accept the principle of telepathy (the communication of thought from one mind to another without the aid of signs, symbols or sounds) as a reality, you of course understand why *enthusiasm* is contagious and why it influences all within its radius.

When your own mind is vibrating at a high rate, because it has been stimulated with *enthusiasm*, that vibration registers in the minds of all within its radius, and especially in the minds of those with whom you come in close contact. When a public speaker 'senses' the feeling that his audience is 'en rapport' with him he merely recognizes the fact that his own *enthusiasm* has influenced the minds of his listeners until their minds are vibrating in harmony with his own.

When the salesman 'senses' the fact that the 'psychological' moment for closing a sale has arrived, he merely feels the effect of his own *enthusiasm* as it influences the mind of his prospective buyer and places that mind 'en rapport' (in harmony) with his own.

The subject of *suggestion* constitutes so vitally an important part of this lesson, and of this entire course, that I will now proceed to describe the three mediums through which it usually operates; namely, what you say, what you do and what you *think!*

When you are enthusiastic over the goods you are selling or the services you are offering, or the speech you are delivering, your state of mind becomes obvious to all who hear you, *by the tone of your voice.*

Whether you have ever thought of it in this way or not, it is the tone in which you make a statement, more than it is the statement itself, that carries conviction or fails to convince. No mere combination of words can ever take the place of a deep belief in a statement that is expressed with burning *enthusiasm*. Words are but devitalized sounds unless coloured with feeling that is born of *enthusiasm*.

Here the printed word fails me, for I can never express with mere type and paper the difference between words that fall from unemotional lips, without the fire of *enthusiasm* hack of them, and those which seem to pour forth from a heart that is bursting with eagerness for expression. The difference is there, however.

Thus, *what you say*, and the way in which you say it, conveys a meaning that may be just the opposite to what is intended. This accounts for many a failure by the salesman who presents his arguments in words which seem logical enough, but lack the colouring that can come only from *enthusiasm* that is born of sincerity and belief in the goods he is trying to sell. His words said one thing, but the tone of his voice *suggested* something entirely different; therefore, no sale was made.

That which you *say* is an important factor in the operation of the principle of *suggestion*, but not nearly so important as that which you do. Your acts will count for more than your words, and woe unto you if the two fail to harmonize.

If a man preaches the Golden Rule as a sound rule of conduct his words will fall upon deaf ears if he does not practice that which he preaches. The most effective sermon that any man can preach on the soundness of the Golden Rule is that which he preaches, by suggestion, when he applies this rule in his relationships with his fellow men.

If a salesman of Ford automobiles drives up to his

prospective purchaser in a Buick, or some other make of car, all the arguments he can present in behalf of the Ford will be without effect. Once I went into one of the offices of the Dictaphone Company to look at a Dictaphone (dictating machine). The salesman in charge presented a logical argument as to the machine's merits, while the stenographer at his side was transcribing letters from a shorthand notebook. His arguments in favour of a dictating machine, as compared with the old method of dictating to a stenographer, did not impress me, because his actions were not in harmony with his words.

Your *thoughts* constitute the most important of the three ways in which you apply the principle of *suggestion*, for the reason that they control the tone of your words and, to some extent at least, your actions. If your *thoughts* and your *actions* and your *words* harmonize, you are bound to influence those with whom you come in contact, more or less toward your way of thinking.

We will now proceed to analyse the subject of *suggestion* and to show you exactly how to apply the principle upon which it operates. As we have already seen, *suggestion* differs from autosuggestion only in one way—we use it, consciously or unconsciously, when we influence others, while we use *autosuggestion* as a means of influencing ourselves.

Before you can influence another person through *suggestion*, that person's mind must be in a state of neutrality; that is, it must be open and receptive to your method of *suggestion*. Right here is where most salesmen fail—they try to make a sale before the mind of the prospective buyer has been rendered receptive or neutralized. This is such a vital point in this lesson that I feel impelled to dwell upon it until there can be no doubt that you understand the principle that I am describing.

When I say that the salesman must neutralize the mind of

his prospective purchaser before a sale can be made I mean that the prospective purchaser's mind must be credulous. A state of confidence must have been established and it is obvious that there can be no set rule for either establishing confidence or neutralizing the mind to a state of openness. Here the ingenuity of the salesman must supply that which cannot be set down as a hard and fast rule.

I know a life insurance salesman who sells nothing but large policies, amounting to $100,000 and upward. Before this man even approaches the subject of insurance with a prospective client he familiarizes himself with the prospective client's complete history, including his education, his financial status, his eccentricities if he has any, his religious preferences and other data too numerous to be listed. Armed with this information, he manages to secure an introduction under conditions which permit him to know the prospective client in a social as well as a business way. Nothing is said about the sale of life insurance during his first visit, nor his second, and sometimes he does not approach the subject of insurance until he has become very well acquainted with the prospective client.

All this time, however, he is not dissipating his efforts. He is taking advantage of these friendly visits for the purpose of neutralizing his prospective client's mind; that is, he is building up a relationship of confidence so that when the time comes for him to talk life insurance that which he says will fall upon ears that *willingly listen.*

Some years ago I wrote a book entitled *How to Sell Your Services.* Just before the manuscript went to the publisher, it occurred to me to request some of the well-known men of the United States to write letters of endorsement to be published in the book. The printer was then waiting for the manuscript; therefore, I hurriedly wrote a letter to some eight or ten men, in which I briefly outlined exactly what I wanted, but the letter brought back no replies. I had failed to observe two important prerequisites for success—I had written the letter so hurriedly that I had failed to inject the spirit of *enthusiasm* into it, and, I had neglected so to word the letter that it had the effect of neutralizing the minds of those to whom it was sent; therefore, I had not paved the way for the application of the principle of *suggestion*.

After I discovered my mistake, I then wrote a letter that was based upon strict application of the principle of suggestion, and this letter not only brought back replies from all to whom it was sent, but many of the replies were masterpieces and served, far beyond my fondest hopes, as valuable supplements to the book.

◆

NOT ALL ADVICE IS GOOD ADVICE

Suggestion is one of the most subtle and powerful principles of psychology. You are making use of it in all that you do and say and think, but, unless you understand the difference between negative suggestion and positive suggestion, you may be using it in such a way that it is bringing you defeat instead of success.

Science has established the fact that through the negative use of suggestion life may be extinguished. Some years ago, in France, a criminal was condemned to death, but before the time for his execution an experiment was performed on him which conclusively proved that through the principle of suggestion death, could be produced. The criminal was brought to the guillotine and his head was placed under the knife, after he had been blindfolded. A heavy, sharp-edged plank was then dropped on his neck, producing a shock similar to that of a sharp-edged knife. Warm water was then gently poured on his neck and allowed to trickle slowly down his spine, to imitate the flow of warm blood. In seven minutes the doctors pronounced the man dead. His imagination, through the principle of suggestion, had actually turned the sharp-edged plank into a guillotine blade and stopped his heart from beating.

In the little town where I was raised, there lived an old lady who constantly complained that she feared death from cancer. During her childhood she had seen a woman who had cancer and the sight had so impressed itself upon her mind that she began to look for the symptoms of cancer in her own body. She was sure that every little ache and pain was the beginning of her long- looked-for symptom of cancer. I have seen her place her hand on her breast and have heard her exclaim, 'Oh, I am sure I have a cancer growing here. I can feel it.' When complaining of this imaginary disease, she always placed her hand on her left breast, where she believed the cancer was attacking her.

For more than twenty years she kept this up.

A few weeks ago she died—*with cancer on her left breast!* If suggestion will actually turn the edge of a plank into a guillotine blade and transform healthy body cells into parasites out of which cancer will develop, can you not imagine what it will do in destroying disease germs, if properly directed? *Suggestion* is the law through which mental healers work what appear to be miracles. I have personally witnessed the removal of parasitical growths known as warts, through the aid of suggestion, within forty-eight hours.

You—the reader of this lesson—can be sent to bed with an *imaginary* sickness of the worst sort, in two hours' time or less, through the use of *suggestion*. If you should start down the street and three or four people in whom you had confidence should meet you and each exclaim that you look ill you would be ready for a doctor.

I wish to take advantage of this appropriate opportunity to state that all of the really big men whom I have had the pleasure of knowing have been the most willing and courteous men of my acquaintance when it came to rendering service that was of benefit to others. Perhaps that was one reason why they were *really* big men.

THE HUMAN MIND IS A MARVELLOUS PIECE OF MACHINERY!

One of its outstanding characteristics is noticed in the fact that all impressions which reach it, either through outside *suggestion* or autosuggestion, are recorded together in groups which harmonize in nature. The negative impressions are stored away, all in one portion of the brain, while the positive impressions are stored in another portion. When one of these impressions (or past experiences) is called into the conscious mind, through the principle of memory, there is a tendency to recall with it all others of a similar nature, just as the raising of one link of a chain brings up other links with it. For example, anything that causes a feeling of doubt to arise in a person's mind is sufficient to call forth all of his experiences which caused him to become doubtful. If a man is asked by a stranger to cash a check, immediately he remembers having cashed checks that were not good, or of having heard of others who did so. Through the law of association all similar emotions, experiences and sense impressions that reach the mind are filed away together, so that the recalling of one has a tendency to bring back to memory all the others.

To arouse a feeling of distrust in a person's mind has a tendency to bring to the surface every doubt-building experience that person ever had. For this reason, successful salesmen endeavour to keep away from the discussion of subjects that may arouse the buyer's 'chain of doubt impressions' which he has stored away by reason of previous experiences. The successful salesman quickly learns that 'knocking' a competitor or a competing article may result in bringing to the buyer's mind certain negative emotions growing out of previous experiences which may make it impossible for the salesman to 'neutralize' the buyer's mind.

This principle applies to and controls every sense impression that is lodged in the human mind. Take the feeling of fear, for example: the moment we permit a single emotion that is related to fear to reach the conscious mind, it calls with it all of its unsavoury relations. A feeling of courage cannot claim the attention of the conscious mind while a feeling of fear is there. One or the other must dominate. They make poor roommates because they do not harmonize in nature. Like attracts like. Every thought held in the conscious mind has a tendency to draw to it other thoughts of a similar nature. You see, therefore, that these feelings, thoughts and emotions growing out of past experiences, which claim the attention of the conscious mind, are backed by a regular army of supporting soldiers of a similar nature, that stand ready to aid them in their work.

Deliberately place in your own mind, through the principle of autosuggestion, the ambition to succeed through the aid of a *definite chief aim*, and notice how quickly all of your latent or undeveloped ability in the nature of past experiences will become stimulated and aroused to action in your behalf. Plant in a boy's mind, through the principle of *suggestion*, the ambition to become a successful lawyer or doctor or engineer or business man or financier, and if you plant that suggestion deeply enough, and keep it there, by repetition, it will begin to move that boy toward the achievement of the object of that ambition.

If you would plant a suggestion 'deeply', mix it generously with enthusiasm, for enthusiasm is the fertilizer that will insure its rapid growth as well as its permanency.

When that kind-hearted old gentleman planted in my mind the suggestion that I was a 'bright boy' and that I could make my mark in the world if I would educate myself, it was not so much *what* he said, as it was the *way in which he said it* that made such a deep and lasting impression on my mind. It was the way in which he gripped my shoulders and the look of confidence in his eyes that drove his suggestion so deeply into my subconscious mind that it never gave me any peace until I commenced taking the steps that led to the fulfilment of the suggestion.

This is a point that I would stress with all the power at my command. *It is not so much what you say as it is the TONE and MANNER in which you say it that makes, a lasting impression.*

It naturally follows, therefore, that sincerity of purpose, honesty and earnestness must be placed back of all that one says if one would make a lasting and favourable impression.

Whatever you successfully sell to others you must first sell to *yourself.*

POINTS TO REMEMBER

1. Enthusiasm is the vital moving force that impels *action.*
2. Thoughts can be influenced through suggestion and autosuggestion.
3. Happiness is the final object of all human effort.

4

CO-OPERATION

Co-operation is the beginning of all organized effort. Andrew Carnegie accumulated a gigantic fortune through the co-operative efforts of a small group of men numbering not more than a score.

You, too, can learn how to use this principle.

There are two forms of Co-operation to which your attention will be directed in this lesson; namely:

First, the Co-operation between people who group themselves together or form alliances for the purpose of attaining a given end, under the principles known as the Law of the Master Mind.

Second, the Co-operation between the conscious and the subconscious minds, which forms a reasonable hypothesis of man's ability to contact, communicate with and draw upon infinite intelligence.

To one who has not given serious thought to this subject, the foregoing hypothesis may seem unreasonable; but follow the evidence of its soundness, study the facts upon which the hypothesis is based and then draw your own conclusions.

Let us begin with a brief review of the physical construction of the body:

'We know that the whole body is traversed by a network of

nerves which serve as the channels of communication between the indwelling spiritual ego, which we call mind, and the functions of the external organism.

'This nervous system is dual. One system, known as the Sympathetic, is the channel for all those activities which are not consciously directed by our volition, such as the operation of the digestive organs, the repair of the daily wear and tear of the tissues and the like.

'The other system, known as the Voluntary or Cerebrospinal system, is the channel through which we receive conscious perception from the physical senses and exercise control over the movements of the body. This system has its centre in the brain, while the other has its centre in the ganglionic mass at the back of the stomach known as the solar plexus, and sometimes spoken of as the abdominal brain. The cerebrospinal system is the channel of our volitional or conscious mental action, and the sympathetic system is the channel of that mental action which unconsciously supports the vital functions of the body.

'Thus the cerebrospinal system is the organ of the conscious mind and the sympathetic is that of the subconscious mind.

'But the interaction of conscious and subconscious minds requires a similar interaction between the corresponding systems of nerves, and one conspicuous connection by which this is provided is the "vagus" nerve. This nerve passes out of the cerebral region as a portion of the voluntary system, and through it we control the vocal organs; then it passes onward to the thorax, sending out branches to the heart and lungs; and finally, passing through the diaphragm, it loses the outer coating which distinguishes the nerves of the voluntary system and becomes identified with those of the sympathetic system, so forming a connecting link between the two and making the man physically a single entity.

'Similarly different areas of the brain indicate their connection with the objective and subjective activities of the mind respectively, and, speaking in a general way, we may assign the frontal portion of the brain to the former, and the posterior portion to the latter, while the intermediate portion partakes of the character of both.

'The intuitional faculty has its correspondence in the upper area of the brain, situated between the frontal and the posterior portions, and, physiologically speaking, it is here that intuitive ideas find entrance. These, at first, are more or less unformed and generalized in character, but are, nevertheless, perceived by the conscious mind; otherwise, we should not be aware of them at all. Then the effort of Nature is to bring these ideas into more definite and usable shape, so the conscious mind lays hold on them and induces a corresponding vibratory current in the voluntary system of nerves, and this in turn induces a similar current in the involuntary system, thus banding the idea over to the subjective mind. The vibratory current which had first descended from the apex of the brain to the frontal brain and thus through the voluntary system to the solar plexus is now reversed and ascends from the solar plexus through the sympathetic system to the posterior brain, this return current indicating the action of the subjective mind.'

If we were to remove the surface portion of the apex of the brain, we should find immediately below it the shining belt of brain substance called the 'corpus callous'. This is the point of union between the subjective and objective, and, as the current returns from the solar plexus to this point, it is restored to the objective portion of the brain in a fresh form which it has acquired by the silent alchemy of the subjective mind. Thus the conception which was at first only vaguely recognized is restored to the objective mind in a definite and workable form, and then the objective mind, acting through the frontal brain—the area of comparison and analysis—proceeds to work upon a clearly perceived idea and to bring out the potentialities that are latent in it.

SUBJECTIVE AND OBJECTIVE MIND

The term 'subjective mind' is the same as the term 'subconscious mind', and the term 'objective mind' is the same as the term 'conscious mind'.

Please understand these different terms.

By studying this dual system through which the body transmits energy, we discover the exact points at which the two systems are connected, and the manner in which we may transmit a thought from the conscious to the subconscious mind.

This co-operative dual nervous system is the most important form of co-operation known to man; for it is through the aid of this system that the principle of evolution carries on its work of developing accurate thought.

When you impress any idea on your sub-conscious mind, through the principle of autosuggestion, you do so with the aid of this dual nervous system, and when your subconscious mind works out a definite plan of any desire with which you impress it, the plan is delivered back to your conscious mind through this same dual nervous system.

This co-operative system of nerves literally constitutes a direct line of communication between your ordinary conscious mind and infinite intelligence.

Knowing, from my own previous experience as a beginner in the study of this subject, how difficult it is to accept the hypothesis here described, I will illustrate the soundness of the hypothesis in a simple way that you can both understand and demonstrate for yourself.

Before going to sleep at night impress upon your mind the desire to arise the next morning at a given hour, say at four a.m., and if your impression is accompanied by a positive determination to arise at that hour, your sub-conscious mind will register the impression and awaken you at precisely that time.

Now the question might well be asked:

'If I ran impress my subconscious mind with the desire to arise at a specified time and it will awaken me at that time, why do I not form the habit of impressing it with other and more important desires?'

We will now take up the subject of co-operation between men who unite, or group themselves together for the purpose of attaining a given end.

This course touches some phase of co-operation in practically every lesson. This result was inevitable for the reason that the object of the course is to help the student develop power, and power is developed only through organised effort.

We are living in an age of co-operative effort. Nearly all successful businesses are conducted under some form of cooperation. The same is true in the field of industry and finance, as well as in the professional field.

Doctors and lawyers have their alliances for mutual aid and protection in the form of Bar Associations and Medical Associations.

The bankers have both local and national Associations for their mutual aid and advancement.

The retail merchants have their Associations for the same purpose.

The automobile owners have grouped themselves into Clubs and Associations.

The Printers have their Associations; the plumbers have theirs and the coal dealers have theirs.

Co-operation is the object of all these Associations.

The labouring men have their unions and those who supply the working capital and superintend the efforts of labouring men have their alliances, under various names.

Nations have their co-operative alliances, although they do not appear to have yet discovered the full meaning of 'co-operation'. The attempt of the late President Wilson to perfect the League of Nations, followed by the efforts of the late President Harding to perfect the same idea under the name of the World Court, indicates the trend of the times in the direction of co-operation.

It is slowly becoming obvious to man that those who most efficiently apply the principle of co-operative effort survive longest, and, that this principle applies from the lowest form of animal life to the highest form of human endeavour.

HOW POWER IS DEVELOPED THROUGH CO-OPERATION

As we have already seen, power is organized effort or energy. Personal power is developed by developing, organizing and coordinating the faculties of the mind. This may be accomplished by mastering and applying the fifteen major principles upon which this course is founded. The necessary procedure through which these principles may be mastered is thoroughly described in the sixteenth lesson.

The development of personal power is but the first step to be taken in the development of the potential power that is available through the medium of allied effort, or co-operation, which may be called group power.

It is a well-known fact that all men who have amassed large fortunes have been known as able 'organizers'. By this is meant that they possessed the ability to enlist the co-operative efforts of other men who supplied talent and ability which they, themselves, did not possess.

The chief object of this course is so to unfold the principles of organized and co-operative or allied effort that the student will comprehend their significance and make them the basis of his philosophy.

Take, as an example, any business or profession that you choose and you will observe, by analysis, that it is limited only by lack of application of organized and co-operative effort. As an illustration, consider the legal profession.

If a law firm consists of but one type of mind it will be greatly handicapped, even though it may be made up of a dozen able men of this particular type. The complicated legal system calls or a greater variety of talent than any one man could possibly provide.

It is evident, therefore, that mere organized effort is not sufficient to ensure outstanding success; the organization must consist of individuals each of whom supplies some specialized talent which the other members of the organization do not possess.

A well-organized law firm would include talent that was specialized in the preparation of cases; men of vision and imagination who understood how to harmonize the law and the evidence of a case under a sound plan. Men who have such ability are not always possessed of the ability to try a case in court; therefore, men who are proficient in court procedure must be available. Carrying the analysis a step further, it will be seen that there are many different classes of cases which call for men of various types of specialized ability in both the preparation and the trial of these cases. A lawyer who had prepared himself as a specialist in corporation law might be wholly unprepared to handle a case in criminal procedure.

In forming a law partnership, the man who understood the principles of organised, co-operative effort, would surround himself with talent that was specialized in every branch of law and legal procedure in which he intended to practice. The man who had no conception of the potential power of these principles would probably select his associates by the usual 'hit or miss' method, basing his selections more upon personality or acquaintanceship than consideration of the particular type of legal talent that each possessed.

The subject of organised effort has been covered in the preceding lessons of this course, but it is again brought up in connection with this lesson for the purpose of indicating the necessity of forming alliances or organizations consisting of individuals who supply all of the necessary talent that may he needed for the attainment of the object in mind.

In nearly all commercial undertakings, there is a need for at least three classes of talent; namely, buyers, salesmen and those who are familiar with finance. It will be readily seen that when these three classes of men organise and co-ordinate their efforts, they avail themselves, through this form of co-operation, of power which no single individual of the group possesses.

Many a business fails because all of the men back of it are salesmen or financial men or buyers. By nature, the most able salesmen are optimistic, enthusiastic and emotional; while able financial men, as a rule, are unemotional, deliberate and conservative. Both classes are essential to the success of a commercial enterprise; but either class will prove too much of a load for any business, without the modifying influence of the other class.

Unfortunate is the person who either through ignorance, or because of egotism, imagines that he can sail this sea of life in the frail bark of independence. Such a person will discover that there are maelstroms more dangerous than any mere whirlpool of unfriendly waters. All natural laws and all of Nature's plans are based upon harmonious, co-operative effort, as all who have attained high places in the world have discovered.

Wherever people are engaged in unfriendly combat, no matter what may be its nature, or its cause, one may observe the nearness of one of these maelstroms that awaits the combatants.

Success in life cannot be attained except through peaceful, harmonious, co-operative effort. Nor can success be attained single-handed or independently. Even though a man may live as a hermit in the wilderness, far from all signs of civilization, he is, nevertheless, dependent upon forces outside of himself for an existence. The more he becomes a part of civilization the more dependent upon co-operative effort he becomes.

Whether a man earns his living by days' work or from the interest on the fortune he has amassed, he will earn it with less opposition through friendly co-operation with others. Moreover, the man whose philosophy is based upon co-operation instead of competition will not only acquire the necessities and the luxuries of life with less effort, but he will enjoy an extra reward in happiness such as others will never feel.

Fortunes that are acquired through co-operative effort inflict no scars upon the hearts of their owners, which is more than can be said of fortunes that are acquired through conflict and competitive methods that border on extortion.

The accumulation of material wealth, whether the object is that of bare existence or luxury, consumes most of the time that we put into this earthly struggle. If we cannot change this materialistic tendency of human nature, we can, at least, change the method of pursuing it by adopting co-operation as the basis of the pursuit.

> **POINTS TO REMEMBER**
> 1. Cooperation is the beginning of all organized effort.
> 2. Power is developed only through organized effort.
> 3. Success in life cannot be attained except through peaceful, harmonious, co-operative effort.

5

INSPIRE TEAMWORK

Cooperation, like love and friendship, is something you get by giving. There are many travellers on the road that leads to happiness. You will need their cooperation, and they will need yours.

And there will be other generations after ours. Their lot in life will depend largely on the inheritance we leave them. We all must become bridge builders, not only for the present generation but for generations yet unborn.

The spirit of unselfish teamwork will provide greater benefits for both you and your generation as well as help those to come. In building a better world for your children, you will be preparing yourself for the better things in life that come as a result of friendly cooperation.

This kind of cooperation has been a major part of the growth of the United States into the most powerful and economically advantaged nation in the world. As Americans we are bound in a common cause, and no matter what misfortunes overtake us, we must shoulder those burdens equally in the spirit of unselfish teamwork if we are to retain our pre-eminence.

Until we become inspired with the spirit of teamwork and recognize the oneness of all people and the fellowship of all humanity, we will not truly benefit from the principle of cooperative effort. Greed and selfishness have no part in this spirit.

In this chapter you will see examples of the power of cooperation at work and learn how to inspire it in the people you work with.

WHAT IS TEAMWORK?

In your mastermind alliance you build a small group of individuals committed to the same definite purpose. You all share the same burning obsession, you each benefit from the increased enthusiasm, imagination and knowledge, and you are in agreement on the division of the rewards of your labour. Teamwork establishes much the same relationship, but since it involves working with people who probably don't have the same burning obsession you do, it requires more effort on your part to maintain a commitment to the work you seek from others and for them to discover their own desires.

Management guru Peter Drucker says that all employees 'have to see themselves as executives,' so that they see the work they do in the context of an entire operation. Managers must learn to subordinate themselves to the work they are doing and not become concerned with promoting their own positions at the expense of their employees. Drucker recalls the example of General Douglas MacArthur, who started every staff meeting with a presentation from the most junior officer present. MacArthur allowed no one to interrupt because he knew it was important to build the confidence of his officers. He wanted and needed that confidence.

Your habit of going the extra mile must extend to your associates. Even if your benefits are generous and your salaries good, people can come to take these things for granted. You should anticipate your associates' needs and act before they even recognize them.

Teamwork sometimes appears among people who are forced by necessity to work together, but it is undependable and never lasts. The United States and the Soviet Union were allies against Hitler, but the alliance evaporated as soon as he was vanquished.

True teamwork depends on relating yourself to others in such a way that they work with you willingly. It is up to you to supply the motives for that willingness and to be alert to any changes in it. Teamwork is a never-ending process, and even though it depends on everyone involved, the responsibility for it lies with you.

TEAMWORK TURNS A COMPANY AROUND

During its early years, the National Cash Register found itself in financial difficulty because a negative attitude had set in among its sales representatives. Hugh Chalmers, the company's sales manager, called his reps together to address this problem.

Chalmers realized that the sales reps were the company's greatest asset, which could be preserved only by restoring the fullest measure of teamwork.

When the reps were assembled, Chalmers stood up in front of them and said, 'Some of our competitors have started a whispering campaign that this company is in such financial difficulty that we will not be able to pull through; there are rumours that we intend to cut our sales force and lay many of you off. This simply is not true.

'Some of you have been influenced by these reports until your sales have dropped off alarmingly. I've brought you here to give you an opportunity to speak for yourselves. I hope you will speak frankly, no matter how you feel.

'The meeting is now open to you. Will each of you please tell what has happened to curtail your sales and what you think we should do to restore that old team spirit which existed before these rumours were spread?'

One of the reps stood up. 'My sales have been dropping off because I have a territory that has been hit hard by drought. Nobody is buying cash registers because their business has suffered. Worse, our competitors are cutting prices and offering deals which make it impossible for me to compete with them.

'And,' the rep continued, 'this is a presidential election year and everyone in my territory is worried about the outcome. No one seems to be interested in buying anything until they know what will be happening in Washington next year.'

A second rep stood up. His story was even more negative than the first one, full of woe and an evident conviction that the company was doomed. He announced boldly that he was looking for another job.

Before he finished, Chalmers jumped up and held out his hand for silence, then exclaimed, 'This meeting will take a fifteen-minute recess while I get my shoes shined. Please remain seated.'

And to the astonishment of the sales force Chalmers sent for the young boy who shined shoes in the company's factory, a common service in those days. Paying no attention to his audience, Chalmers chatted with the boy.

At the end of the conversation Chalmers handed the boy a dime and then announced that the youngster was going to make a speech.

No one could have been more surprised than the shoeshine boy. 'I don't know how to make a speech,' he protested.

'Yes, you do,' Chalmers replied. 'And you can make a better one than the last two we heard. I'll help you.

'How old are you?' Chalmers asked.

'Eleven,' the boy replied.

'How long have you been shining shoes in this plant?'

'Six months.'

'Good! How much do you get for shining shoes?'

'I get a nickel,' the boy replied, 'but sometimes I get another for tips, like you gave me.'

'Who had your job before you did?'

'It was a boy named Ted.'

'And how old was he?' Chalmers queried.

'Seventeen.'

'Do you know why he left?'

'I heard he thought he couldn't make a living.'

'Can you make a living at a nickel a shine?' Chalmers asked.

'Oh yes, sir. I give my mother ten dollars on Friday, and I put five dollars in the bank, and I have two dollars left for spending money. Some weeks I make more than that. I'm saving on the side to buy a bicycle, but my mother doesn't know anything about that.'

'Thank you,' Chalmers said. 'You have made a very fine speech. '

Turning to his audience, Chalmers said, 'You have heard this boy's story. Now let me tell you want it means.

'In the first place, I want to call your attention to the fact that this boy is doing a job that used to be held by someone six years older than he, doing the same work, charging the same price and serving the same people who work in this plant.

'The older boy quit this job because he couldn't make a living from it, but this boy not only has money for himself and his dreams but helps support his family. He is working the same territory older boy worked, but he is working it in a different mental attitude.

'He is cooperative; he goes about his work with a smile on his face; he expects success, and he is finding it. The older boy was indifferent, moody and never took the trouble to say "thank you" when his patrons handed him a nickel. Therefore, that was all they did hand him; no tips, no great amount of repeat orders for his services. Of course, he couldn't make a living. Furthermore—'

At this point Chalmers was interrupted by a rep. 'I get the point! Those of us who have been failing in the field have been buying other people's hard-luck stories instead of selling them cash registers. I know that is what I've been doing. I've been trying to do my job with a negative mind, and that's why my sales have fallen off. I don't know how anyone else feels about it, but I'm going back to my territory and start working it as I never worked it before. I can promise you that in the future you will get orders for cash registers from me instead of hard luck stories.'

Another rep jumped up and cried, 'That goes for me, too!' Then another. Soon pandemonium broke out with everyone talking at the same time. The conference wound up that night with a banquet at which every sales rep promised to return to the field with a new spirit of faith.

The year that followed was one of the most profitable in the history of NCR. What happened? A leader had seen what it was his workers needed. In this case it was a kick in the pants that showed them that success is something you create for yourself, not something others steal from you. Chalmers refired their dedication to their tasks with a vivid example of the success that was available to anyone committed to its pursuit.

Although he strongly suspected what ailed his reps, he was wise enough to give them the opportunity to express their concerns; Chalmers knew he needed a frank working relationship with his force. He didn't punish those who had the courage to speak up. He offered every one of them, complainer or not, the same thing: a vision of what he could accomplish. And he started his speech with the reassurance that the company was standing behind its sales force.

Chalmers maintained a positive attitude in his relations with his reps, and he influenced them to respond in kind.

Teamwork costs so little in time and effort, and it pays huge dividends. One wonders why so many people go out of their way to make life miserable for themselves and others by failing to realize this.

TEAMWORK AS A MODEL FOR BUSINESS

Years ago, an article by Robert Littell in Reader's Digest described a management system in use by the McCormick spice company in Baltimore. This system was revolutionary in its time, though more and more companies have now adopted something similar. McCormick called it 'the multiple management plan', which is just another way of saying 'teamwork'.

When Charles P. McCormick succeeded his uncle as head of the company, he decided to share the responsibilities of running the show with those who could be taught to take it. He picked seventeen young people from the company's front office and made them the Junior Board of Directors. They were charged with examining and discussing everything the company did, then presenting their findings to the regular board—as long as they were unanimous in their decision.

As Littell wrote, 'A flood of energy and new ideas was released. Men who had felt themselves to be merely glorified clerks tasted responsibility and clamoured for more. Even in the first year and a half practically all of the Juniors' recommendations were adopted.'

The same policy was applied to the assembly line, where a Factory Board was formed with the same charge. The three boards met together weekly in a spirit of harmony, everyone seeking ways to improve business and efficiency, to raise McCormick another notch higher.

McCormick's personnel policy was truly forward-thinking. Dismissing a worker required the signatures of four superiors who thought the action was necessary, and anyone threatened with dismissal was allowed to plead his or her case. As Littell noted, 'McCormick & Company charges itself with an error if it lets a man go until he has been helped to see that his going is just and necessary…'

The multiple management plan worked for McCormick & Company because of the spirit of human understanding and teamwork the individual workers put into it—a spirit which began with management and was readily embraced by the employees. And obviously this spirit of understanding and teamwork served to provide sound economies in the management of the company because it recognized and appropriately awarded merit, down to the humblest employee, and at the same time eliminated the unwilling and unfit from the organization.

People will work harder for personal recognition and a word of commendation where it is deserved than they will for money alone. No one wants to feel as if he or she is merely a cog in a wheel. Your job as a leader is to see that everyone has a role in your group or organization and that he or she recognizes the importance of that role.

Through the multiple management plan McCormick put the soul back into its firm and provided every worker with a very real desire and worthwhile motive to go the extra mile and to do it with a positive mental attitude. That is the essence of teamwork.

There is no record of anyone's ever having made a great contribution to civilization without the cooperation of others. Even great artists like Michelangelo depended upon assistants, craftsmen and patrons to make their work possible.

There is a state of mind that tends to make people akin, establishes rapport between minds and provides the power of attraction that gains the friendly teamwork of others. This state of mind, like so many of the other priceless assets of life, is usually attained by the concentration of the mind on attaining a definite major purpose backed by an appropriate motive and self-discipline.

That state is enthusiasm. It is contagious. Infect others with your enthusiasm, and teamwork will be the inevitable result.

POINTS TO REMEMBER

1. To be happy you need other people's cooperation and also give them in return.
2. The spirit of unselfish teamwork will provide greater benefits.
3. Teamwork is a never-ending process, and even though it depends on everyone involved, the responsibility for it lies with you.

6

HOW TO MOTIVATE YOURSELF

What is motivation?

Motivation is that which *induces action* or *determines choice*. It is that which *provides a motive*. A motive is the 'inner urge' *only within the individual* which incites him to action, such as an instinct, passion, emotion, habit, mood, impulse, desire or idea.

It is the hope or *other force* which starts an action in an attempt to produce specific results.

Motivating yourself and others. When you know principles that *can* motivate you, you will then know principles that *can* motivate others. Conversely, when you know principles that *can* motivate others, you will then know principles that *can* motivate you.

My purpose in illustrating specific experiences of the success and failures of others is to motivate you to desirable action.

Now, therefore, to motivate yourself, try to understand principles that motivate others—to motivate others, try to understand principles that motivate you.

Establish the habit of motivating yourself with PMA…at will. And then you can direct your thoughts, control your emotions, and ordain your destiny.

Motivate yourself and others with the magic ingredient. What is the magic ingredient?

One man, in particular, found it. Here is his story.

Some years ago, this man, a successful cosmetic manufacturer, retired at the age of sixty-five. Each year thereafter his friends gave him a birthday party, and on each occasion, they asked him to disclose his formula. Year after year he pleasantly refused; however, on his seventy-fifth birthday his friends, half-jokingly and half seriously, once again asked if he would disclose the secret.

'You have been so wonderful to me over the years that I now will tell you,' he said. 'You see, in addition to the formulas used by other cosmeticians, I added the magic ingredient.'

'What is the magic ingredient?' he was asked.

'I never promised a woman that my cosmetics would make her beautiful, but I always gave her hope.'

HOPE IS A MAGIC INGREDIENT!

Hope is a desire with the expectation of obtaining what is desired and belief that it is obtainable. A person consciously reacts to that which to him is desirable, believable and attainable.

And he also subconsciously reacts to the inner urge that induces action when environmental suggestion, self-suggestion or autosuggestion cause the release of the powers of his subconscious mind. His response to suggestion may develop obedience that is direct, neutral or in reverse action to a specific symbol. In other words, there may be various types and degrees of motivating factors.

Every result has a given cause. Your every act is the result of a given cause—your motives.

Hope, for example, motivated the cosmetic manufacturer to build a profitable business. Hope also motivated women to buy his cosmetics. Hope will motivate you, too.

The ten basic motives which inspire all human action. Every thought you think, every act in which you voluntarily engage, can be traced back to some definite motive or combination of motives. There are ten basic motives which inspire all thoughts, all voluntary actions. No one ever does anything without having been motivated to do it.

When it comes to learning how to motivate yourself for any given purpose, or how to motivate others, you should have a clear understanding of these ten basic motives. Here they are:

1. The desire for SELF-PRESERVATION
2. The emotion of LOVE
3. The emotion of FEAR
4. The emotion of SEX
5. The desire for LIFE AFTER DEATH
6. The desire for FREEDOM OF BODY AND MIND
7. The emotion of ANGER
8. The emotion of HATE
9. The desire for RECOGNITION and SELF-EXPRESSION
10. The desire for MATERIAL GAIN

As you have been reading this chapter, perhaps you felt that it contains food for thought. A good sandwich contains nine-tenths bread and one-tenth meat. Unlike a sandwich, this chapter is nine-tenths meat. That is the way the authors planned it. We hope you will chew and digest it carefully.

Are negative emotions good? Negative emotions, feelings and thoughts are harmful to the individual. But are there times when these are good?

Yes, negative emotions, feelings, thoughts and attitudes are good—at the proper time and under the right circumstances.

For that which is good for the species of man is good for the individual. It is clear that in the process of evolution, negative thoughts, feelings, emotions and attitudes protected the individual. In fact, these negatives prevented the species of man from becoming extinct. And these negatives in a person, like the negative forces of a bar magnet, effectively repelled the forces of the negative powers of others. This has been. And because it is a universal law, it will continue to be.

Now culture, refinement and civilization, like man himself, have also evolved from a primitive state. And the more cultured, refined and civilized a society or environment may be, the less need there is for the individual to use these negatives. But in a negative, antagonistic environment, a person with common sense will use these negative forces with PMA to oppose the evil with which he is faced.

And because you live in a country with laws designed to bring the greatest good to the greatest number; because the rights of the individual are protected; because you are in a society and environment of culture, refinement and the highest form of civilization, those negative thoughts, feelings, emotions and passions which lie dormant within you from your hereditary past are not now necessary to solve the problems which primitive man could not otherwise have solved. For he was a law unto himself. And the law of the individual has become subservient to the law of society for his benefit.

Now let's clarify these concepts. Let's take anger, hate and fear as examples.

Anger and hate. Righteous indignation against evil is a form of anger and hate. The desire to protect one's nation when attacked by an enemy, or the desire to protect the weak against the criminal attack of the madman to save human life is good. To kill to accomplish this, when necessary, is an example of the worst form of all negative feelings and emotions used to achieve a worthy purpose. In our society the patriotism of a soldier or the fulfilment of duty by a police officer are virtues.

Fear. With every new experience and in every new environment nature protects you from potential danger by alerting you through some shade of the emotion of fear. You can be assured that the bravest individual will, in a new environment, at first, experience an awareness that is a conscious or subconscious feeling of timidity or fear. If he finds that the fears are not beneficial to him, the person with PMA will neutralize an undesirable negative emotion by substituting a positive one.

What can you do about it? Man is the only member of the animal kingdom who, through the functioning of his conscious mind, can voluntarily control his emotions from within, rather than be forced to do so by external influences.

And he alone can deliberately change habits of emotional response. The more civilized, cultured and refined you are, the more easily you can control your emotions and feelings if you choose to do so.

Emotions are controlled through the combination of reason and action. When fears are unwarranted, or harmful, they can and should be neutralized.

How?

While your emotions are not always immediately subject to reason, nonetheless they are immediately subject to action. For you can use reason to determine the needlessness of the negative emotion and thus motivate yourself to action. You can substitute fear with a positive feeling. How do you do this?

FORMULA THAT GUARANTEES DISCIPLINE

One effective means is through self-suggestion, in fact self-command, with a one-word symbol that incorporates what you want to be. Thus, if you are afraid and want to be courageous, give the self-command *be courageous* with rapidity several times. Follow this with action. If you want to be courageous, act courageously.

How?

Use the self-starter *Do it Now!* And then get into action.

Keep your mind on the things you should and do want and off the things you shouldn't and don't want.

A success formula that always succeeds when applied. Are you among the hundreds of thousands of persons throughout the world who have read the *Autobiography of Benjamin Franklin*, or among the tens of thousands who have read Frank Bettger's book *How I Raised Myself from Failure to Success in Selling*? If not, I recommend that you read both. These books contain a formula that always succeeds when applied with PMA.

In his autobiography, Franklin indicates that he endeavoured to help Benjamin Franklin just as the most important living person wants to help you. He wrote (language modernized):

'My intention being to acquire the habit of all these virtues, I judged it would be well not to distract my attention by attempting the whole at once, but to fix it on one of them at a time; and when I should be master of that, then to proceed to another, and so on, until I should have gone through the thirteen, and, as the previous acquisition of some might facilitate the acquisition of certain others, I arranged them with that view...'

The names of these virtues as Franklin listed them, together with the precepts (self-motivators for self-suggestion) he gave each one, are:

1.	TEMPERANCE	Eat not to dullness; drink not to elevation.
2.	SILENCE	Speak not but what may benefit others or yourself; avoid trifling conversation.
3.	ORDER	Let all your things have their places; let each part of your business have its time.
4.	RESOLUTION	Resolve to perform what you ought; perform without fail what you resolve.
5.	FRUGALITY	Make no expense but to do good to others or yourself, that is, waste nothing.
6.	INDUSTRY	Lose no time; be always employed in something useful; cut off all unnecessary actions.
7.	SINCERITY	Use no hurtful deceit; think innocently and justly, and, if you speak, speak accordingly.
8.	JUSTICE	Wrong none by doing injuries, or omitting the benefits that are your duty.
9.	MODERATION	Avoid extremes; forbear resenting injuries so much as you think they deserve.
10.	CLEANLINESS	Tolerate no uncleanliness in body, clothes or habitation.
11.	TRANQUILITY	Be not disturbed at trifles, or at accidents, common or unavoidable.
12.	CHASTITY	Rarely use venery but for health or offspring, never to dullness, weakness, or the injury of your own or another's peace or reputation.
13.	HUMILITY	Imitate Jesus and Socrates.

Franklin wrote further, 'Conceiving then that, agreeably to the advice of Pythagoras in his Golden Verses, daily examination would be necessary, I contrived the following method for conducting that examination.'

Now it is as important to know how to use a formula as it is to know the formula. Here's how to use your knowledge:

A formula in action:

1. *Concentrate on one principle for an entire week,* every day of the week. Respond by proper action every time an occasion arises.
2. And then, start the second week on the second principle or virtue. Let the first be taken over by your subconscious.

POINTS TO REMEMBER

1. Hope is the primary force for motivation.
2. Start motivating others around you as well.
3. When fears are unwarranted, or harmful, they can and should be neutralized.

7

SELF-CONFIDENCE

Scepticism is the deadly enemy of progress and self-development. You might as well lay this book aside and stop right here as to approach this lesson with the feeling that it was written by some longhaired theorist who had never tested the principles upon which the lesson is based.

Surely this is no age for the sceptic, because it is an age in which we have seen more of Nature's laws uncovered and harnessed than had been discovered in all past history of the human race. Within three decades we have witnessed the mastery of the air; we have explored the ocean; we have all hut annihilated distances on the earth; we have harnessed the lightning and made it turn the wheels of industry; we have made seven blades of grass grow where but one grew before; we have instantaneous communication between the nations of the world. Truly, this is an age of illumination and unfoldment, but we have as yet barely scratched the surface of knowledge. However, when we shall have unlocked the gate that leads to the secret power which is stored up within us it will bring us knowledge that will make all past discoveries pale into oblivion by comparison.

Thought is the most highly organized form of energy known to man, and this is an age of experimentation and research that is sure to bring us into greater understanding of that mysterious force called thought, which reposes within us. We have already found out enough about the human mind to know that a man may throw off the accumulated effects of a thousand generations of *fear*, through the aid of the principle of *autosuggestion*. We have already discovered the fact that fear is the chief reason for poverty and failure and misery that takes on a thousand different forms. We have already discovered the fact that the man who masters *fear* may march on to successful achievement in practically any undertaking, despite all efforts to defeat him.

The development of self-confidence starts with the elimination of this demon called fear, which sits upon a man's shoulder and whispers into his ear, '*You can't do it——you are afraid to try——you are afraid of public opinion——you are afraid that you will fail——you are afraid you have not the ability.*' This *fear* demon is getting into close quarters. Science has found a deadly weapon with which to put it to flight, and this lesson on *self-confidence* has brought you this weapon for use in your battle with the world-old enemy of progress, *fear*.

THE SIX BASIC FEARS OF MANKIND: every person falls heir to the influence of six basic fears. Under these six fears may be listed the lesser fears. The six basic or major fears are here enumerated and the sources from which they are believed to have grown are described. The six basic fears are:

a. The fear of Poverty
b. The fear of Old Age
c. The fear of Criticism
d. The fear of Loss of Love of Someone

e. The fear of Ill Health
   f. The fear of Death.

Study the list, then take inventory of your own fears and ascertain under which of the six headings you can classify them.

Every human being who has reached the age of understanding is bound down, to some extent, by one or more of these six basic fears. As the first step in the elimination of these six evils let us examine the sources from whence we inherited them.

PHYSICAL AND SOCIAL HEREDITY

All that man is, both physically and mentally, he came by through two forms of heredity. One is known as physical heredity and the other is called social heredity.

Through the law of physical heredity man has slowly evolved from the amoeba (a single-cell animal form), through stages of development corresponding to all the known animal forms now on this earth, including those which are known to have existed but which are now extinct.

Every generation through which man has passed has added to his nature something of the traits, habits and physical appearance of that generation. Man's physical inheritance, therefore, is a heterogeneous collection of many habits and physical forms.

There seems little, if any, doubt that while the six basic fears of man could not have been inherited through physical heredity (these six basic fears being mental states of mind and therefore not capable of transmission through physical heredity), it is obvious that through physical heredity a most favourable lodging place for these six fears has been provided.

For example, it is a well-known fact that the whole process

of physical evolution is based upon death, destruction, pain and cruelty; that the elements of the soil of the earth find transportation, in their upward climb through evolution, based upon the death of one form of life in order that another and higher form may subsist. All vegetation lives by 'eating' the elements of the soil and the elements of the air. All forms of animal life live by 'eating' some other and weaker form, or some form of vegetation.

The cells of all vegetation have a very high order of intelligence. The cells of all animal life likewise have a very high order of intelligence.

Undoubtedly the animal cells of a fish have learned, out of bitter experience, that the group of animal cells known as a fish hawk are to be greatly feared.

By reason of the fact that many animal forms (including that of most men) live by eating the smaller and weaker animals, the 'cell intelligence' of these animals which enter into and become a part of man brings with it the FEAR growing out of their experience in having been eaten alive.

This theory may seem to be far-fetched, and in fact it may not be true, but it is at least a logical theory if it is nothing more. The author makes no particular point of this theory, nor does he insist that it accounts for any of the six basic fears. There is another, and a much better explanation of the source of these fears, which we will proceed to examine, beginning with a description of social heredity.

By far the most important part of man's make-up comes to him through the law of social heredity, this term having reference to the methods by which one generation imposes upon the minds of the generation under its immediate control the superstitions, beliefs, legends and ideas which it, in turn, inherited from the generation preceding.

The term 'social heredity' should be understood to mean any and all sources through which a person acquires knowledge, such as schooling of religious and all other natures; reading, word of mouth conversation, storytelling and all manner of thought inspiration coming from what is generally accepted as one's 'personal experiences'.

Through the operation of the law of social heredity anyone having control of the mind of a child may, through intense teaching, plant in that child's mind any idea, whether false or true, in such a manner that the child accepts it as true and it becomes as much a part of the child's personality as any cell or organ of its physical body (and just as hard to change in its nature).

It is through the law of social heredity that the religionist plants in the child mind dogmas and creeds and religious ceremonies too numerous to describe, holding those ideas before that mind until the mind accepts them and forever seals them as a part of its irrevocable belief.

The mind of a child which has not come into the age of general understanding, during an average period covering, let us say, the first two years of its life, is plastic, open, clean and free. Any idea planted in such a mind by one in whom the child has confidence takes root and grows, so to speak, in such a manner that it never can be eradicated or wiped out, no matter how opposed to logic or reason that idea may be.

Many religionists claim that they can so deeply implant the tenets of their religion in the mind of a child that there never can be room in that mind for any other religion, either in whole or in part. The claims are not greatly overdrawn.

With this explanation of the manner in which the law of social heredity operates the student will be ready to examine the sources from which man inherits the six basic fears. Moreover, any student (except those who have not yet grown big enough to examine truth that steps upon the 'pet corns' of their own superstitions) may check the soundness of the principle of social heredity as it is here applied to the six basic fears, without going outside of his or her own personal experiences.

Fortunately, practically the entire mass of evidence submitted in this lesson is of such a nature that all who sincerely seek the truth may ascertain, for themselves, whether the evidence is sound or not.

For the moment at least, lay aside your prejudices and preconceived ideas (you may always go back and pick them up again, you know) while we study the origin and nature of man's Six Worst Enemies, the six basic fears, beginning with:

The Fear of Poverty: it requires courage to tell the truth about the origin of this fear, and still greater courage, perhaps, to accept the truth after it has been told. The fear of poverty grew out of man's inherited tendency to prey upon his fellow man economically. Nearly all forms of lower animals have instinct but appear not to have the power to reason and think; therefore, they prey upon one another physically. Man, with his superior sense of intuition, thought and reason, does not eat his fellow men bodily; he gets more satisfaction out of eating them FINANCIALLY!

Of all the ages of the world of which we know anything, the age in which we live seems to be the age of money worship. A man is considered less than the dust of the earth unless he can display a fat bank account. Nothing brings man so much suffering and humiliation as does POVERTY. No wonder man FEARS poverty. Through a long line of inherited experiences with the man-animal man has learned, for certain, that this animal cannot always be trusted where matters of money and other evidences of earthly possessions are concerned.

Many marriages have their beginning (and oftentimes their ending) solely on the basis of the wealth possessed by one or both of the contracting parties. It is no wonder that the divorce courts are busy!

'Society' could quite properly be spelled '$ociety', because it is inseparably associated with the dollar mark. So eager is man to possess wealth that he will acquire it in whatever manner he can; through legal methods, if possible, through other methods if necessary.

The fear of poverty is a terrible thing!

A man may commit murder, engage in robbery, rape and all other manner of violation of the rights of others and still regain a high station in the minds of his fellow men, PROVIDING always that he does not lose his wealth. Poverty, therefore, is a crime—an unforgivable sin, as it were.

No wonder man fears it!

Every statute book in the world bears evidence that the fear of poverty is one of the six basic fears of mankind, for in every such book of laws may be found various and sundry laws intended to protect the weak from the strong. To spend time trying to prove either that the fear of poverty is one of man's inherited fears, or that this fear has its origin in man's nature to cheat his fellow man, would be similar to trying to prove that three times two are six. Obviously, no man would ever fear poverty if he had any grounds for trusting his fellow men, for there is food and shelter and raiment and luxury of every nature sufficient for the needs of every person on earth, and all these blessings would be enjoyed by every person except for the swinish habit that man has of trying to push all the other 'swine' out of the trough, even after he has all and more than he needs.

The second of the six basic fears with which man is bound is:

The Fear of Old Age: in the main this fear grows out of two sources. First, the thought that Old Age may bring with it POVERTY. Secondly, and by far the most common source of origin, from false and cruel sectarian teachings which have been so well mixed with 'fire and brimstone' and with 'purgatories' and other bogies that human beings have learned to fear Old Age because it meant the approach of another, and possibly a much more HORRIBLE, world than this one which is known to be bad enough.

In the basic fear of Old Age man has two very sound reasons for his apprehension: the one growing out of distrust of his fellow men who may seize whatever worldly goods he may possess, and the other arising from the terrible pictures of the world to come which were deeply planted in his mind, through the law of social heredity, long before he came into possession of that mind.

Is it any wonder that man fears the approach of Old Age?

The third of the six basic fears is:

The Fear of Criticism: just how man acquired this basic fear it would be hard, if not impossible, definitely to determine, but one thing is certain, he has it in well-developed form.

Some believe that this fear made its appearance in the mind of man about the time that politics came into existence. Others believe its source can be traced no further than the first meeting of an organization of females known as a 'Woman's club'. Still another school of humourists charges the origin to the contents of the Holy Bible, whose pages abound with some very vitriolic and violent forms of criticism. If the latter claim is correct, and those who believe literally all they find in the Bible are not mistaken, then God is responsible for man's inherent fear of

Criticism, because God caused the Bible to be written.

This author, being neither a humourist nor a 'prophet', but just an ordinary workaday type of person, is inclined to attribute the basic fear of Criticism to that part of man's inherited nature which prompts him not only to take away his fellow man's goods and wares, but to justify his action by CRITICISM of his fellow man's character.

The fear of Criticism takes on many different forms, the majority of which are petty and trivial in nature, even to the extent of being childish in the extreme.

Bald-headed men, for example, are bald for no other reason than their fear of Criticism. Heads become bald because of the protection of hats with tight fitting bands which cut off the circulation at the roots of the hair. Men wear hats, not because they actually need them for the sake of comfort, but mainly because 'everybody's doing it', and the individual falls in line and does it also, lest some other individual CRITICIZE him.

Women seldom have bald heads, or even thin hair, because they wear hats that are loose, the only purpose of which is to make an appearance.

But it must not be imagined that women are free from the fear of Criticism associated with hats. If any woman claims to be superior to man with reference to this fear, ask her to walk down the street wearing a hat that is one or two seasons out of style!

The makers of all manner of clothing have not been slow to capitalize this basic fear of Criticism with which all mankind is cursed. Every season, it will be observed, the 'styles' in many articles of wearing apparel change. Who establishes the 'styles'? Certainly not the purchaser of clothes, but the manufacturer of clothes. Why does he change the styles so often? Obviously, this change is made so that the manufacturer can sell more clothes.

For the same reason the manufacturers of automobiles (with a few rare and very sensible exceptions) change styles every season.

The manufacturer of clothing knows how the man-animal fears to wear a garment which is one season out of step with 'that which they are all wearing now'.

Is this not true? Does not your own experience back it up? We have been describing the manner in which people behave under the influence of the fear of Criticism as applied to the small and petty things of life. Let us now examine human behaviour under this fear when it affects people in connection with the more important matters connected with human intercourse. Take, for example, practically any person who has reached the age of 'mental maturity' (from thirty-five to forty-five years of age, as a general average), and if you could read his or her mind you would find in that mind a very decided disbelief of and rebellion against most of the fables taught by the majority of the religionists. Powerful and mighty is the fear of CRITICISM!

The time was, and not so very long ago at that, when the word 'infidel' meant ruin to whomsoever it was applied. It is seen, therefore, that man's fear of CRITICISM is not without ample cause for its existence.

The fourth basic fear is that of:

The Fear of the Loss of Love: the source from which this fear originated needs but little description, for it is obvious that it grew out of man's nature to steal his fellow man's mate; or at least to take liberties with her, unknown to her rightful 'lord' and master. By nature, all men are polygamous, the statement of a truth which will, of course, bring denials from those who are either too old to function in a normal way sexually, or have, from some other cause, lost the contents of certain glands which are responsible for man's tendency toward the plurality of the opposite sex.

There can be but little doubt that jealousy and all other similar forms of more or less mild *dementia praecox* (insanity) grew out of man's inherited fear of the Loss of Love of Someone.

Of all the 'sane fools' studied by this author, that represented by a man who has become jealous of some woman, or that of a woman who has become jealous of some man, is the oddest and strangest. The author, fortunately, never had but one case of personal experience with this form of insanity, but from that experience he learned enough to justify him in stating that the fear of the Loss of Love of Someone is one of the most painful, if not in fact the most painful, of all the six basic fears. And it seems reasonable to add that this fear plays more havoc with the human mind than do any of the other six basic fears, often leading to the more violent forms of permanent insanity.

The fifth basic fear is that of:

The Fear of Ill Health: this fear has its origin, to considerable extent also, in the same sources from which the fears of Poverty and Old Age are derived.

The fear of Ill Health must needs be closely associated with both Poverty and Old Age, because it also leads toward the border line of 'terrible worlds' of which man knows not, but of which he has heard some discomforting stories.

The author strongly suspects that those engaged in the business of selling good health methods have had considerable to do with keeping the fear of Ill Health alive in the human mind.

For longer than the record of the human race can be relied upon, the world has known of various and sundry forms of therapy and health purveyors. If a man gains his living from keeping people in good health it seems but natural that he would use every means at his command for persuading people that they needed his services. Thus, in time, it might be that people would inherit a fear of Ill Health.

The sixth and last of the six basic fears is that of:

The Fear of Death: to many this is the worst of all the six basic fears, and the reason why it is so regarded becomes obvious to even the casual student of psychology.

The terrible pangs of fear associated with DEATH may be charged directly to religious fanaticism, the source which is more responsible for it than are all other sources combined.

So-called 'heathen' are not as much afraid of DEATH as are the 'civilized', especially that portion of the civilized population which has come under the influence of theology.

For hundreds of millions of years man has been asking the still unanswered (and, it may be, the unanswerable) questions, 'WHENCE?' and 'WHITHER?' 'Where did I come from and where am I going after death?'

The more cunning and crafty, as well as the honest but credulous, of the race have not been slow to offer the answer to these questions. In fact, the answering of these questions has become one of the so-called 'learned' professions, despite the fact that but little learning is required to enter this profession. Witness, now, the major source of origin of the fear of DEATH!

'Come into my tent, embrace my faith, accept my dogmas (and pay my salary) and I will give you a ticket that will admit you straightway into heaven when you die,' says the leader of one form of sectarianism. 'Remain out of my tent,' says this same leader, 'and you will go direct to hell, where you will burn throughout eternity.'

While, in fad, the self-appointed leader may not be able to

provide safe-conduct into heaven nor, by lack of such provision, allow the unfortunate seeker after truth to descend into hell, the possibility of the latter seems so terrible that it lays hold of the mind and creates that fear of fears, the fear of DEATH!

In truth no man knows, and no man has ever known, what heaven or hell is like, or if such places exist, and this very lack of definite knowledge opens the door of the human mind to the charlatan to enter and control that mind with his stock of legerdemain and various brands of trickery, deceit and fraud.

The truth is this—nothing less and nothing more—That NO MAN KNOWS NOR HAS ANY MAN EVER KNOWN WHERE WE COME FROM AT BIRTH OR WHERE WE GO AT DEATH. Any person claiming otherwise is either deceiving himself or he is a conscious impostor who makes it a business to live without rendering service of value, through play upon the credulity of humanity.

WORDS OF WISDOM FOR THE WIVES

I am going to digress and here and break the line of thought for a moment while recording a word of advice to the wives of men. Remember, these lines are intended only for wives, and husbands are not expected to read that which is here set down.

From having analysed more than 16,000 people, the majority of whom were married men, I have learned something that may be of value to wives. Let me state my thought in these words:

You have it within your power to send your husband away to his work or his business or his profession each day with a feeling of self-confidence that will carry him successfully over the rough spots of the day and bring him home again, at night, smiling and happy. One of my acquaintances of former years married a woman who had a set of false teeth. One day his wife dropped her teeth and broke the plate. The husband picked up the pieces and began examining them. He showed such interest in them that his wife said, 'You could make a set of teeth like those if you made up your mind to do it.'

This man was a farmer whose ambitions had never carried him beyond the bounds of his little farm until his wife made that remark. She walked over and laid her hand on his shoulder and encouraged him to try his hand at dentistry. She finally coaxed him to make the start, and today he is one of the most prominent and successful dentists in the state of Virginia. I know him well, for he is my father!

No one can foretell the possibilities of achievement available to the man whose wife stands at his back and urges him on to bigger and better endeavour, for it is a well-known fact that a woman can arouse a man so that he will perform almost superhuman feats. It is your right and your duty to encourage your husband and urge him on in worthy undertakings until he shall have found his place in the world. You can induce him to put forth greater effort than can any other person in the world. Make him believe that nothing within reason is beyond his power of achievement and you will have rendered him a service that will go a long way toward helping him win in the battle of life.

One of the most successful men in his line in America gives entire credit for his success to his wife. When they were first married, she wrote a creed which he signed and placed over his desk. This is a copy of the creed:

I believe in myself. I believe in those who work with me. I believe in my employer. I believe in my friends. I believe in my family. I believe that God will lend me everything I need with which to succeed if I do my best to earn it through faithful and honest service. I believe in prayer and I will never close my eyes in sleep without praying for divine guidance to the end that I will be patient with other people and tolerant with those who do not believe as I do. I believe that success is the result of intelligent effort and does not depend upon luck or sharp practices or double-crossing friends, fellow men or my employer. I believe I will get out of life exactly what I put into it, therefore I will be careful to conduct myself toward others as I would want them to act toward me. I will not slander those whom I do not like. I will not slight my work no matter what I may see others doing. I will render the best service of which I am capable because I have pledged myself to succeed in life and I know that success is always the result of conscientious and efficient effort. Finally, I will forgive those who offend me because I realise that I shall sometimes offend others and I will need their forgiveness.

Signed ....

The woman who wrote this creed was a practical psychologist of the first order. With the influence and guidance of such a woman as a helpmate any man could achieve noteworthy success.

Analyse this creed and you will notice how freely the personal pronoun is used. It starts off with the affirmation of self-confidence, which is perfectly proper. No man could make this creed his own without developing the positive attitude that would attract to him people who would aid him in his struggle for success.

This would be a splendid creed for every salesman to adopt. It might not hurt your chances for success if *you* adopted it. Mere adoption, however, is not enough. You must *practice* it! Read it over and over until you know it by heart. Then repeat it at least once a day until you have literally transformed it into your mental make-up. Keep a copy of it before you as a daily reminder of your pledge to practice it. By doing so you will be making efficient use of the principle of autosuggestion as a means of developing self-confidence. Never mind what anyone may say about your procedure. Just remember that it is your business to succeed, and this creed, if mastered and applied, will go a long way toward helping you.

You might well remember that *nothing can bring you success but yourself.* Of course, you will need the co-operation of others if you aim to attain success of a far-reaching nature, but you will never get that cooperation unless you vitalize your mind with the positive attitude of self-confidence.

We come, now, to the point at, which you are ready to take hold of the principle of autosuggestion and make direct use of it in developing yourself into a positive and dynamic and self-reliant person. You are instructed to copy the following formula, sign it and commit it to memory:

SELF-CONFIDENCE FORMULA

First: I know that I have the ability to achieve the object of my *definite purpose*, therefore I *demand* of myself persistent, aggressive and continuous action toward its attainment.

Second: I realize that the dominating thoughts of my mind eventually reproduce themselves in outward, bodily action and gradually transform themselves into physical reality, therefore I will concentrate my mind for thirty minutes daily upon the task of thinking of the person I intend to be, by creating a mental picture of this person and then transforming that picture into reality through practical service.

Third: I know that through the principle of autosuggestion, any desire that I persistently hold in my mind will eventually seek expression through some practical means of realizing it, therefore I shall devote ten minutes daily to demanding of myself the development of the factors named in the sixteen lessons of this Reading Course on the Law of Success.

Fourth: I have clearly mapped out and written down a description of my *definite purpose* in life, for the coming five years. I have set a price on my services for each of these five years; a price that I intend to *earn* and *receive*, through strict application of the principle of efficient, satisfactory service which I will render in advance.

Fifth: I fully realize that no wealth or position can long endure unless built upon truth and justice, therefore *I will engage in no transaction which does not benefit all whom it affects.* I will succeed by attracting to me the forces I wish to use, and the co-operation of other people. I will induce others to serve me because I will first serve them. I will eliminate hatred, envy, jealousy, selfishness and cynicism by developing love for all humanity, because I know that a negative attitude toward others can never bring me success. I will cause others to *believe in me* because I will believe in them and in myself.

I will sign my name to this formula, commit it to memory and repeat it aloud once a day with full *faith* that it will gradually influence my entire life so that I will become a successful and happy worker in my chosen field of endeavour.

Signed ....

Before you sign your name to this formula make sure that you intend to carry out its instructions. Back of this formula lies a law that no man can explain. The psychologists refer to this law as autosuggestion and let it go at that, but you should bear in mind one point about which there is no uncertainty, and that is the fact that whatever this law is it *actually works!*

Another point to be kept in mind is the fact that, just as electricity will turn the wheels of industry and serve mankind in a million other ways, or snuff out life if wrongly applied, so will this principle of autosuggestion lead you up the mountain-side of peace and prosperity, or down into the valley of misery and poverty, according to the application you make of it. If you fill your mind with doubt and unbelief in your ability to achieve, then the principle of autosuggestion takes this spirit of unbelief and sets it up in your subconscious mind as your dominating thought *and slowly but surely draws you into the whirlpool of failure.* But, if you fill your mind with radiant self-confidence, the principle of autosuggestion takes this belief and sets it up as your dominating thought and helps you master the obstacles that fall in your way until you reach the mountain-top of *success.*

THE POWER OF HABIT

Having, myself, experienced all the difficulties that stand in the road of those who lack the understanding to make practical application of this great principle of autosuggestion, let me take you a short way into the principle of habit, through the aid of which you may easily apply the principle of autosuggestion in any direction and for any purpose whatsoever.

Habit grows out of environment; out of doing the same thing or thinking the same thoughts or repeating the same words over and over again. Habit may be likened to the groove on a phonograph record, while the human mind may be likened to the needle that fits into that groove. When any habit has been well formed, through repetition of thought or action, the mind has a tendency to attach itself to and follow the course of that habit as closely as the phonograph needle follows the groove in the wax record.

Habit is created by *repeatedly* directing one or more of the five senses of seeing, hearing, smelling, tasting and feeling, in a given direction. It is through this repetition principle that the injurious drug habit is formed. It is through this same principle that the desire for intoxicating drink is formed into a habit.

After habit has been well established it will automatically control and direct our bodily activity, wherein may be found a thought that can be transformed into a powerful factor in the development of *self-confidence*. The thought is this: I v*oluntarily, and by force if necessary, direct your efforts and your thoughts along a desired line until you have formed the habit that will lay hold of you and continue, voluntarily, to direct your efforts along the same line.*

The object in writing out and repeating the self-confidence formula is to form the habit of making *belief in yourself* the dominating thought of your mind until that thought has been thoroughly imbedded in your subconscious mind, through the principle of *habit*.

You learned to write by repeatedly directing the muscles of your arm and hand over certain outlines known as letters, until finally you formed the habit of tracing these outlines. Now you write with ease and rapidity, without tracing each letter slowly. Writing has become a *habit* with you.

The principle of habit will lay hold of the faculties of your mind just the same as it will influence the physical muscles of your body, as you can easily prove by mastering and applying this lesson on

Self-confidence. Any statement that you repeatedly make to yourself, or any *desire* that you deeply plant in your mind through repeated statement, will eventually seek expression through your physical, outward bodily efforts. The principle of habit is the very foundation upon which this lesson on self-confidence is built, and if you will understand and follow the directions laid down in this lesson you will soon know more about the law of habit, from first-hand knowledge, than could be taught you by a thousand such lessons as this.

You have but little conception of the possibilities which lie sleeping within you, awaiting but the awakening hand of vision to arouse you, and you will never have a better conception of those possibilities unless you develop sufficient Self-confidence to lift you above the commonplace influences of your present environment.

The human mind is a marvellous, mysterious piece of machinery, a fact of which I was reminded a few months ago when I picked up Emerson's Essays and re-read his essay on Spiritual Laws. A strange thing happened. I saw in that essay, which I had read scores of times previously, much that I had never noticed before. I saw more in this essay than I had seen during previous readings because the unfoldment of my mind since the last reading had prepared me to interpret more.

The human mind is constantly unfolding, like the petals of a flower, until it reaches the maximum of development. What this maximum is, where it ends, or whether it ends at all or not, are unanswerable questions, but the degree of unfoldment seems to vary according to the nature of the individual and the degree to which he keeps his mind at work. A mind that is forced or coaxed into analytical thought every day seems to keep on unfolding and developing greater powers of interpretation.

Down in Louisville, Kentucky, lives Mr Lee Cook, a man who has practically no legs and has to wheel himself around on a cart. In spite of the fact that Mr Cook has been without legs since birth, he is the owner of a great industry and a millionaire through his own efforts. He has proved that a man can get along very well without legs if he has a well-developed self-confidence.

In the city of New York, one may see a strong able-bodied and able-headed young man, without legs, rolling himself down Fifth Avenue every afternoon, with cap in hand, begging for a living. His head is perhaps as sound and as able to think as the average.

This young man could duplicate anything that Mr Cook, of Louisville, has done, if *he thought of himself as Mr Cook thinks of himself.*

Henry Ford owns more millions of dollars than he will ever need or use. Not so many years ago, he was working as a labourer in a machine shop, with but little schooling and without capital. Scores of other men, some of them with better organized brains than his, worked near him. Ford threw off the poverty consciousness, developed confidence in himself, thought of success and attained it. Those who worked around him could have done as well had they *thought* as he did.

Milo C. Jones, of Wisconsin, was stricken down with paralysis a few years ago. So bad was the stroke that he could not turn himself in bed or move a muscle of his body. His physical body was useless, but there was nothing wrong with his brain, so it began to function in earnest, probably for the first time in its existence. Lying flat on his back in bed, Mr Jones made that brain create a *definite purpose.* That purpose was prosaic and humble enough in nature, but it was *definite* and it was a *purpose*, something that he had never known before.

His *definite purpose* was to make pork sausage. Calling his family around him he told of his plans and began directing them in carrying the plans into action. With nothing to aid him except a sound mind and plenty of *self-confidence,* Milo C. Jones spread the name and reputation of 'Little Pig Sausage' all over the United States, and accumulated a fortune besides.

All this was accomplished after paralysis had made it impossible for him to work with his hands.

Where *thought* prevails power may be found!

Henry Ford has made millions of dollars and is still making millions of dollars each year because *he believed in Henry Ford* and transformed that belief into a *definite purpose* and backed that purpose with a definite plan. The other machinists who worked along with Ford, during the early days of his career, visioned nothing but a weekly pay envelope and that was all they ever got. They demanded nothing out of the ordinary of themselves. If you want to *get more* be sure to *demand* more of yourself. Notice that this demand is to be made on *yourself!*

POINTS TO REMEMBER

1. Scepticism is the deadly enemy of self-development.
2. Thought is the most highly organized form of energy known to man.
3. Fear is the chief reason for poverty and failure.

8

THE GOLDEN RULE

There is more power wrapped up in the preceding lessons of this course than most men could trust themselves with; therefore, this lesson is a governor that will, if observed and applied, enable you to steer your ship of knowledge over the rocks and reefs of failure that usually beset the pathway of all who come suddenly into possession of power.

For more than twenty-five years I have been observing the manner in which men behave themselves when in possession of power, and I have been forced to the conclusion that the man who attains it in any other than by the slow, step-by-step process, is constantly in danger of destroying himself and all whom he influences.

It must have become obvious to you, long before this, that this entire course leads to the attainment of *power* of proportions which may be made to perform the seemingly 'impossible'. Happily, it becomes apparent that this power can only be attained by the observance of many fundamental principles all of which converge in this lesson, which is based upon a law that both equals and transcends in importance every other law outlined in the preceding lessons.

Likewise, it becomes apparent to the thoughtful student that this *power* can endure only by faithful observance of the law upon which this lesson is based, wherein lies the 'safety-valve' that protects the careless student from the dangers of his own follies; and protects, also, those whom he might endanger if he tried to circumvent the injunction laid down in this lesson.

To 'prank' with the power that may be attained from the knowledge wrapped up in the preceding lessons of this course, without a full understanding and strict observance of the law laid down in this lesson, is the equivalent of 'pranking' with a power which may destroy as well as create.

I am speaking, now, not of that which I suspect to be true, but of that which I KNOW TO BE TRUE! The truth upon which this entire course, and this lesson in particular, is founded, is no invention of mine. I lay no claim to it except that of having observed its unvarying application in the everyday walks of life over a period of more than twenty-five years of struggle; and, of having appropriated as much of it as, in the light of my human frailties and weaknesses, I could make use of.

If you demand *positive* proof of the soundness of the laws upon which this course in general, and this lesson in particular, is founded, I must plead inability to offer it except through one witness, and that is *yourself.*

You may have *positive* proof only by testing and applying these laws for yourself.

If you demand more substantial and authoritative evidence than my own, then I am privileged to refer you to the teachings and philosophy of Christ, Plato, Socrates, Epictetus, Confucius, Emerson and two of the more modern philosophers, James and Münsterberg, from whose works I have appropriated all that constitutes the more important fundamentals of this lesson, with the exception of that which I have gathered from my own limited experience.

For more than four thousand years men have been preaching the Golden Rule as a suitable rule of conduct among men, but unfortunately the world has accepted the letter while totally missing the spirit of this Universal Injunction. We have accepted the Golden Rule philosophy merely as a sound rule of ethical conduct but we have failed to understand the law upon which it is based.

I have heard the Golden Rule quoted scores of times, but I do not recall having ever heard an explanation of the law upon which it is based, and not until recent years did I understand that law, from which I am led to believe that those who quoted it did not understand it.

The Golden Rule means, substantially, to do unto others as you would wish them to do unto you if your positions were reversed.

But why? What is the *real* reason for this kindly consideration of others?

The real reason is this:

There is an eternal law through the operation of which we reap that which we sow. When you select the rule of conduct by which you guide yourself in your transactions with others, you will be fair and just, very likely, if you know that you are setting into motion, by that selection, a *power* that will run its course for weal or woe in the lives of others, returning, finally, to help or to hinder you, according to its nature.

'Whatsoever a man soweth that shall be also reap!'

It is your privilege to deal unjustly with others, but, if you understand the law upon which the Golden Rule is based, you must know that your unjust dealings will 'come home to roost'.

If you fully understood the principles described in Lesson Eleven, on *accurate thought*, it will be quite easy for you to understand the law upon which the Golden Rule is based. You cannot pervert or change the course of this law, *but you can adapt yourself to its nature and thereby use it as an irresistible power that will carry you to heights of achievement which could not be attained without its aid.*

This law does not stop by merely flinging back upon you your acts of injustice and unkindness toward others; it goes further than this—much further—and returns to you the results of every *thought* that you release.

Therefore, not alone is it advisable to 'do unto others as you wish them to do unto you', but to avail yourself fully of the benefits of this great Universal Law you must 'think of others as you wish them to think of you'.

The law upon which the Golden Rule is based begins affecting you, either for good or evil, the moment you release a *thought*. It has amounted almost to a worldwide tragedy that people have not generally understood this law. Despite the simplicity of the law it is practically all there is to be learned that is of enduring value to man, for it is the medium through which we become the masters of our own destiny.

Understand this law and you understand *all* that the Bible has to unfold to you, for the Bible presents one unbroken chain of evidence in support of the fact that man is the maker of his own destiny; and, that his *thoughts* and *acts* are the tools with which he does the *making*.

During ages of less enlightenment and tolerance than that of the present, some of the greatest thinkers the world has ever produced have paid with their lives for daring to uncover this Universal Law so that it might be understood by all. In the light of the past history of the world, it is an encouraging bit of evidence, in support of the fact that men are gradually throwing off the veil of ignorance and intolerance, to note that I stand in no danger of bodily harm for writing that which would have cost me my life a few centuries ago.

◆

While this course deals with the highest laws of the universe, which man is capable of interpreting, the aim, nevertheless, has been to show how these laws may be used in the practical affairs of life. With this object of practical application in mind, let us now proceed to analyse the effect of the Golden Rule through the following incident.

THE POWER OF PRAYER

'No,' said the lawyer, 'I shan't press your claim against that man; you can get someone else to take the case, or you can withdraw it; just as you please.'

'Think there isn't any money in it?'

'There probably would be some little money in it, but it would come from the sale of the little house that the man occupies and calls his home! But I don't want to meddle with the matter, anyhow.'

'Got frightened out of it, eh?'

'Not at all.'

'I suppose likely the fellow begged hard to be let off?'

'Well, yes, he did.'

'And you caved in, likely?'

'Yes.'

'What in creation did you do?'

'I believe I shed a few tears.'

'And the old fellow begged you hard, you say?'

'No, I didn't say so; he didn't speak a word to me.'

'Well, may I respectfully inquire whom he did address in your hearing?'

'God Almighty.'

'Ah, he took to praying, did he?'

'Not for my benefit, in the least. You see, I found the little house easily enough and knocked on the outer door, which stood ajar; but nobody heard me, so I stepped into the little hall and saw through the crack of a door a cozy sitting-room, and there on the bed, with her silver head high on the pillows, was an old lady who looked for all the world just like my mother did the last time 1 ever saw her on earth. Well, I was on the point of knocking, when she said, "Come, father, now begin; I'm all ready." And down on his knees by her side went an old, white-haired man, still older than his wife, I should judge, and I couldn't have knocked then, for the life of me. Well, he began. First, he reminded God they were still His submissive children, mother and he, and no matter what He saw fit to bring upon them they shouldn't rebel at His will. Of course, 'twas going to be very hard for them to go out homeless in their old age, especially with poor mother so sick and helpless, and, oh! how different it all might have been if only one of the boys had been spared. Then his voice kind of broke, and a white hand stole from under the coverlet and moved softly over his snowy hair. Then he went on to repeat that nothing could be so sharp again as the parting with those three sons—unless mother and he should be separated.

'But, at last, he fell to comforting himself with the fact that the dear Lord knew that it was through no fault of his own that mother and he were threatened with the loss of their dear little home, which meant beggary and the alms-house—a place they prayed to be delivered from entering if it should be consistent with God's will. And then he quoted a multitude of promises concerning the safety of those who put their trust in the Lord. In fact, it was the most thrilling plea to which I ever listened. And at last, he prayed for God's blessing on those who were about to demand justice.'

The lawyer then continued, more lowly than ever, 'And I—believe—I'd rather go to the poor-house myself tonight than to stain my heart and hands with the blood of such a prosecution as that.'

'Little afraid to defeat the old man's prayer, eh?'

'Bless your soul, man, you couldn't defeat it!' said the lawyer. 'I tell you he left it all subject to the will of God; but he claimed that we were told to make known our desires unto God; but of all the pleadings I ever heard that beat all. You see, I was taught that kind of thing myself in my childhood. Anyway, why was I sent to bear that prayer? I am sure I don't know, but I hand the case over.'

'I wish,' said the client, twisting uneasily, 'you hadn't told me about the old man's prayer.'

'Why so?'

'Well, because I want the money the place would bring; but I was taught the Bible straight enough when I was a youngster and I'd hate to run counter to what you tell about. I wish you hadn't heard a word about it, and, another time, I wouldn't listen to petitions not intended for my ears.'

The lawyer smiled.

'My dear fellow,' he said, 'you're wrong again. It was intended for my ears, and yours, too; and God Almighty intended it. My old mother used to sing about God's moving in a mysterious way, as I remember it.'

'Well, my mother used to sing it, too,' said the claimant, as he twisted the claim-papers in his fingers.

'You can call in the morning, if you like, and tell "mother" and "him" the claim has been met.'

'In a mysterious way,' added the lawyer, smiling.

Neither this lesson nor the course of which it is a part is based upon an appeal to maudlin sentiment, but there can be no escape from the truth that *success*, in its highest and noblest form, brings one, finally, to view all human relationships with a feeling of deep emotion such as that which this lawyer felt when he overheard the old man's prayer.

If may be an old-fashioned idea, but somehow, I can't get away from the belief that *no man can attain success in its highest form without the aid of earnest prayer!*

Prayer is the key with which one may open the secret doorway. In this age of mundane affairs, when the uppermost thought of the majority of people is centred upon the accumulation of wealth, or the struggle for a mere existence, it is both easy and natural for us to overlook the power of earnest prayer.

I am not saying that you should resort to prayer as a means of solving your daily problems which press for immediate attention; no, I am not going that far in a course of instruction which will be studied largely by those who are seeking in it the road to *success* that is measured in dollars; but, may I not modestly suggest to *you* that you, at least, give *prayer* a trial after *everything else Jails* to bring you a *satisfying success?*

Thirty men, red-eyed and dishevelled, lined up before the judge of the San Francisco police court. It was the regular morning company of drunks and disorderlies. Some were old and hardened; others hung their heads in shame. Just as the momentary disorder attending the bringing in of the prisoners quieted down, a strange thing happened. A strong, clear voice from below began singing'

'Last night I lay a-sleeping,
There came a dream so fair.'

'Last night!' It had been for them all a nightmare or a

drunken stupor. The song was such a contrast to the horrible fact that no one could fail of a sudden shock at the thought the song suggested.

'I stood in old Jerusalem,
Beside the Temple there,'

The song went on. The judge had paused. He made a quiet inquiry. A former member of a famous opera company known all over the country was awaiting trial for forgery. It was he who was singing in his cell.

Meantime the song went on, and every man in the line showed emotion. One or two dropped on their knees; one boy at the end of the line, after a desperate effort at self-control, leaned against the wall, buried his face against his folded arms, and sobbed, 'Oh, mother, mother.'

The sobs, cutting to the very heart the men who heard, and the song, still welling its way through the court-room, blended in the hush. At length one man protested. 'Judge,' said he, 'have we got to submit to this? We're here to take our punishment, but this—' He, too, began to sob.

It was impossible to proceed with the business of the court; yet the court gave no order to stop the song. The police sergeant, after an effort to keep the men in line, stepped back and waited with the rest. The song moved on to its climax:

'Jerusalem, Jerusalem!
Sing, for the night is o'er!
Hosanna, in the highest!
Hosanna, for evermore!'

In an ecstasy of melody the last words rang out, and then there was silence. The judge looked into the faces of the men before him. There was not one who was not touched by the song; not one in whom some better impulse was not stirred. He did not call the cases singly—a kind word of advice, and he dismissed them all. No man was fined or sentenced to the workhouse that morning. The song had done more good than *punishment* could possibly have accomplished.

You have read the story of a Golden Rule lawyer and a Golden Rule judge. In these two commonplace incidents of everyday life you have observed how the Golden Rule works when *applied.*

A passive attitude toward the Golden Rule will bring no results; it is not enough merely to *believe* in the philosophy, while, at the same time, failing to *apply* it in your relationships with others. If you want results you must take an *active* attitude toward the Golden Rule. A mere passive attitude, represented by belief in its soundness, will avail you nothing.

Nor will it avail you anything to proclaim to the world your belief in the Golden Rule while your actions are not in harmony with your proclamation. Conversely stated, it will avail you nothing to appear to practice the Golden Rule, while, at heart, you are willing and eager to use this universal law of right conduct as a cloak to cover up a covetous and selfish nature. Murder will out. Even the most ignorant person will 'sense' you for what you are.

'Human character does evermore publish itself. It will not be concealed. It hates darkness—it rushes into light... I heard an experienced counsellor say that he never feared the effect upon a jury of a lawyer who does not believe in his heart that his client ought to have a verdict. If he does not believe it, his unbelief will appear to the jury, despite all his protestations and will become their unbelief. This is that law whereby a work of art, of whatever kind, sets us in the same state of mind wherein the artist was when he made it. That which we do not believe we cannot *adequately say,* though we may repeat the words ever so often. It was this conviction which Swedenborg expressed when he described a group of persons in the spiritual world endeavouring in vain to articulate a proposition which they did not believe; but they could not, though they twisted and folded their lips even to indignation.

'A man passes for what he is worth. What he is engraves itself on his face, on his form, on his fortunes, in letters of light which all men may read but himself... If you would not be known to do anything, never do it. A man may play the fool in the drifts of a desert, but every grain of sand shall seem to see.'—Emerson.

It is the law upon which the Golden Rule philosophy is based to which Emerson has reference in the foregoing quotation. It was this same law that he had in mind when he wrote the following, 'Every violation of truth is not only a sort of suicide in the liar, but is a stab at the health of human society. On the most profitable lie the course of events presently lays a destructive tax; whilst frankness proves to be the best tactics, for it invites frankness, puts the parties on a convenient footing and makes their business a friendship. Trust men and they will be true to you; treat them greatly and they will show themselves great, though they make an exception in your favour to all their rules of trade.'

◆

The Golden Rule philosophy is based upon a law which no man can circumvent. This law is the same law that is described in Lesson Eleven, on Accurate Thought, through the operation of which one's thoughts are transformed into reality corresponding exactly to the nature of the thoughts.

'Once grant the creative power of our thought and there is an end of struggling for our own way, and an end of gaining it *at someone else's expense;* for, since by the terms of the hypothesis we can create what we like, the simplest way of getting what we want is, not to snatch it from somebody else, but to make it for ourselves; and, since there is no limit to thought there can be no need for straining, and for everyone to have his own way in *this manner*, would be to banish all strife, want, sickness, and sorrow from the earth.'

'Now, it is precisely on this assumption of the creative power of our thought that the whole Bible rests. If not, what is the meaning of being saved by Faith? Faith is essentially thought; and, therefore, every call to have faith in God is a call to trust in the power of our own thought about God. "According to your faith be it unto you," says the Old Testament. The entire book is nothing but one continuous statement of the creative power of Thought.

'The Law of Man's Individuality is, therefore, the Law of Liberty, and equally it is the Gospel of peace; for when we truly understand the law of our own individuality, we see that the same law finds its expression in everyone else; and, consequently, we shall reverence *the law in others* exactly in proportion as we value it in ourselves. To do this is to follow the Golden Rule of doing to others what we would they should do unto us; and because we know that the Law of Liberty in ourselves must include the free use of our creative power, there is no longer any inducement to infringe the rights of others, for we can satisfy all our desires by the exercise of our knowledge of the law.

'As this comes to be understood, co-operation will take the place of competition, with the result of removing all ground for enmity, whether between individuals, classes or nations...'

(The foregoing quotation is from Bible Mystery and Bible Meaning by the late Judge T. Troward, published by Robert McBride & Company, New York City. Judge Troward was the author of several interesting volumes, among them The Edinburgh Lectures, which is recommended to all students of this course.)

If you wish to know what happens to a man when he totally disregards the law upon which the Golden Rule philosophy is based, pick out any man in your community whom you know to live for the single dominating purpose of accumulating wealth, and who has no conscientious scruples as to how he accumulates that wealth. Study this man and you will observe that there is no warmth to his soul; there is no kindness to his words; there is no welcome to his face. He has become a slave to the desire for wealth; he is too busy to enjoy life and too selfish to wish to help others enjoy it. He walks, and talks, and breathes, but he is nothing but a human automaton. Yet there are many who envy such a man and wish that they might occupy his position, foolishly believing him to be a *success*.

There can never be *success* without happiness, and no man can be happy without dispensing happiness to others. Moreover, the dispensation must be voluntary and with no other object in view than that of spreading sunshine into the hearts of those whose hearts are heavy-laden with burdens.

George D. Herron had in mind the law upon which the Golden Rule philosophy is based when he said, 'We have talked much of the brotherhood to come; but brotherhood has always been the fact of our life, long before it became a modern and inspired sentiment. Only we have been brothers in slavery and torment, brothers in ignorance and its perdition, brothers in disease, and war, and want, brothers in prostitution and hypocrisy. What happens to one of us sooner or later happens to all; we have always been unescapably involved in common destiny. The world constantly tends to the level of the down most man in it; and that down most man is the world's real ruler, hugging it close to his bosom, dragging it down to his death. You do not think so, but it is true, and it ought to be true. For if there were some way by which some of us could get free, apart from others, if there were some way by which some of us could have heaven while others had hell, if there were some way by which part of the world could escape some form of the blight and peril and misery of disinherited labour, then indeed would our world be lost and damned; but since men have never been able to separate themselves from one another's woes and wrongs, since history is fairly stricken with the lesson that we cannot escape brotherhood of some kind, since the whole of life is teaching us that we are hourly choosing between brotherhood in suffering and brotherhood in good, it remains for us to choose the brotherhood of a co-operative world, with all its fruits thereof—the fruits of *love* and *liberty.*

LEARN TO LIVE AND LET LIVE

The world war ushered us into an age of co-operative effort in which the law of 'live and let live' stands out like a shining star to guide us in our relationships with each other. This great universal call for co-operative effort is taking on many forms, not the least important of which are the Rotary Clubs, the Kiwanis Clubs, the Lions Clubs and the many other luncheon clubs which bring men together in a spirit of friendly intercourse, for these clubs mark the beginning of an age of friendly competition in business. The next step will be a closer alliance of all such clubs in an out-and-out spirit of friendly cooperation.

The attempt by Woodrow Wilson and his contemporaries to establish the League of Nations, followed by the efforts of Warren G. Harding to give footing to the same cause under the name of the World Court, marked the first attempt in the history of the world to make the Golden Rule effective as a common meeting ground for the nations of the world.

There is no escape from the fact that the world has awakened to the truth in George D. Herron's statement that 'we are hourly choosing between brotherhood in suffering and brotherhood in good.' The world war has taught us—nay, forced upon us—the truth that a part of the world cannot suffer without injury to the whole world. These facts are called to your attention, not in the nature of a preachment on morality, but for the purpose of directing your attention to the underlying law through which these changes are being brought about. For more than four thousand years the world has been thinking about the Golden Rule philosophy, and that *thought* is now becoming transformed into realization of the benefits that accrue to those who apply it.

Still mindful of the fact that the student of this course is interested in a material success that can be measured by bank balances, it seems appropriate to suggest here that all who will may profit by shaping their business philosophy to conform with this sweeping change toward co-operation which is taking place all over the world.

If you can grasp the significance of the tremendous change that has come over the world since the close of the world war, and if you can interpret the meaning of all the luncheon clubs and other similar gatherings which bring men and women together in a spirit of friendly co-operation, surely your imagination will suggest to you the fact that this is an opportune time to profit by adopting this spirit of friendly co-operation as the basis of your own business or professional philosophy.

Stated conversely, it must be obvious to all who make any pretence of thinking accurately, that the time is at hand when failure to adopt the Golden Rule as the foundation of one's business or professional philosophy is the equivalent of economic suicide.

◆

Perhaps you have wondered why the subject of *honesty* has not been mentioned in this course, as a prerequisite to *success,* and, if so, the answer will be found in this lesson. The Golden Rule philosophy, when rightly understood and applied, makes dishonesty impossible. It does more than this—it makes impossible all the other destructive qualities such as selfishness, greed, envy, bigotry, hatred and malice.

When you apply the Golden Rule, you become, at one and the same time, both the judge and the judged—the accused and the accuser. This places one in a position in which *honesty* begins in one's own heart, toward one's self, and extends to all others with equal effect. *Honesty* based upon the Golden Rule is not the brand of honesty which recognizes nothing but the question of expediency.

It is no credit to be honest, when honesty is obviously the most *profitable* policy, lest one lose a good customer or a valuable client or be sent to jail for trickery. But when honesty means either a temporary or a permanent material loss, then it becomes an *honour* of the highest degree to all who practice it. Such honesty has its appropriate reward in the accumulated power of character and reputation enjoyed, by all who deserve it.

Those who understand and apply the Golden Rule philosophy are always scrupulously honest, not alone out of their desire to be just with others, but because of their desire to be just with themselves. They understand the eternal law upon which the Golden Rule is based, and they know that through the operation of this law *every thought thy release and every act in which they indulge has its counterpart in some fact or circumstance with which they will later be confronted.*

Golden Rule philosophers are honest because they understand the truth that honesty adds to their own character that 'vital something' which gives it life and power. Those who understand the law through which the Golden Rule operates would poison their own drinking water as quickly as they would indulge in acts of injustice to others, for they know that such injustice starts a chain of causation that will not only bring them physical suffering, but will destroy their characters, stain for ill their reputations and render impossible the attainment of enduring success.

The law through which the Golden Rule philosophy operates is none other than the law through which the principle of Autosuggestion operates. This statement gives you a suggestion from which you should be able to make a deduction of a far-reaching nature and of inestimable value.

Test your progress in the mastery of this course by analysing the foregoing statement and determining, before you read on, what suggestion it offers you.

Of what possible benefit could it be to you to know that when you do unto others as if you were the others, which is the sum and substance of the Golden Rule, you are putting into motion a chain of causation through the aid of a law which affects the others according to the nature of your act, *and at the same time planting in your character, through your subconscious mind, the effects of that act.*

This question practically suggests its own answer, but as I am determined to cause you to think this vital subject out for yourself I will put the question in still another form, viz.: if all your acts toward others, and even your thoughts of others, are registered in your subconscious mind, through the principle of autosuggestion, thereby building your own character in exact duplicate of your *thoughts* and *acts,* can you not see how important it is to guard those acts and thoughts?

We are now in the very heart of the real reason for doing unto others as we would have them do unto us, for it is obvious that whatever we do unto others we do unto ourselves.

Stated in another way, every *act* and every *thought* you release modifies your own character in exact conformity with the nature of the act or thought, and your character is a sort of centre of magnetic attraction which attracts to you the people and conditions that harmonize with it.

You cannot indulge in an act toward another person without having first created the nature of that act in your own *thought, and you cannot release a thought without planting the sum and substance and nature of it in your own sub-conscious mind, there to become a part and parcel of your own character.*

Grasp this simple principle and you will understand why you cannot afford to hate or envy another person. You will also understand why you cannot afford to strike back, in kind, at those who do you an injustice. Likewise, you will understand the injunction, 'Return good for evil.'

Understand the law upon which the Golden Rule injunction is based and you will understand, also, the law that eternally binds all mankind in a single bond of fellowship and renders it impossible for you to injure another person, by *thought ox deed,* without injuring yourself; and, likewise, adds to your own character the results of every kind *thought* and *deed* in which you indulge.

Understand this law and you will then know, beyond room for the slightest doubt, that you are constantly punishing yourself for every wrong you commit and rewarding yourself for every act of constructive conduct in which you indulge.

It seems almost an act of Providence that the greatest wrong and the most severe injustice ever done me by one of my fellow men was done just as I began this lesson. (Some of the students of this course will know what it is to which I refer.)

This injustice has worked a temporary hardship on me, but that is of little consequence compared to the advantage it has given me by providing a timely opportunity for me to test the soundness of the entire premise upon which this lesson is founded.

The injustice to which I refer left two courses of action open to me. I could have claimed relief by 'striking back' at my antagonist, through both civil court action and criminal libel proceedings, or I could have stood upon my right to forgive him. One course of action would have brought me a substantial sum—of money and whatever joy and satisfaction there may be in defeating and *punishing* an enemy. The other course of action would have brought me self-respect which is enjoyed by those who have successfully met the test and discovered that they have evolved to the point at which they can repeat the Lord's Prayer and *mean it!*

I chose the latter course. I did so, despite the recommendations of close personal friends to 'strike back', and despite the offer of a prominent lawyer to do my 'striking' for me *without cost.*

But the lawyer offered to do the impossible, for the reason that no man can 'strike back' at another *without cost.* Not always is the cost of a monetary nature, for there are other things with which one may pay that are dearer than money.

It would be as hopeless to try to make one who was not familiar with the law upon which the Golden Rule is based understand why I refused to strike back at this enemy as it would to try to describe the law of gravitation to an ape. If you understand this law you understand, also, why I chose to *forgive* my enemy.

In the Lord's Prayer we are admonished to forgive our enemies, but that admonition will fall on deaf ears except where the listener understands the law upon which it is based. That law is none other than the law upon which the Golden Rule is based. It is the law that forms the foundation of this entire lesson, and through which we must inevitably reap that which we sow. There is no escape from the operation of this law, nor is there any cause to try to avoid its consequences if we refrain from putting into motion *thoughts* and *acts* that are destructive.

That we may more concretely describe the law upon which this lesson is based, let us embody the law in a code of ethics such as one who wishes to follow literally the injunction of the Golden Rule might appropriately adopt, as follows.

MY CODE OF ETHICS

I. I believe in the Golden Rule as the basis of all human conduct; therefore, I will never do to another person that which I would not be willing for that person to do to me if our positions were reversed.

II. I will be honest, even to the slightest detail, in all my transactions with others, not alone because of my desire to be fair with them, but because of my desire to impress the idea of honesty on my own subconscious mind, thereby weaving this essential quality into my own character.

III. I will forgive those who are unjust toward me, with no thought as to whether they deserve it or not, because I understand the law through which forgiveness of others strengthens my own character and wipes out the effects of my own transgressions, in my subconscious mind.

IV. I will be just, generous and fair with others always, even though I know that these acts will go unnoticed and unrecorded, in the ordinary terms of reward, because I understand and intend to apply the law through the aid of which one's own character is but the sum total of one's own *acts* and *deeds*.

V. Whatever time I may have to devote to the discovery and exposure of the weaknesses and faults of others I will devote, more profitably, to the discovery and *correction* of my own.

VI. I will slander no person, no matter how much I may believe another person may deserve it, because I wish to plant no destructive suggestions in my own subconscious mind.

VII. I recognize the power of Thought as being an inlet leading into my brain from the universal ocean of life; therefore, I will set no destructive thoughts afloat upon that ocean lest they pollute the minds of others.

VIII. I will conquer the common human tendency toward hatred, and envy, and selfishness, and jealousy, and malice, and pessimism, and doubt and fear; for I believe these to be the seed from which the world harvests most of its troubles.

IX. When my mind is not occupied with thoughts that tend toward the attainment of my *definite chief aim* in life, I will voluntarily keep it filled with thoughts of courage, and self-confidence, and goodwill toward others, and faith, and kindness, and loyalty and love for truth and justice, for I believe these to be the seed from which the world reaps its harvest of progressive growth.

X. I understand that a mere passive belief in the soundness of the Golden Rule philosophy is of no value whatsoever, either to myself or to others; therefore, I will *actively* put into operation this universal rule for good in all my transactions with others.

XI. I understand the law through the operation of which my own character is developed from my own *acts* and *thoughts*; therefore, I will guard with care all that goes into its development.

XII. Realizing that enduring happiness comes only through helping others find it; that no act of kindness is without its reward, even though it may never be directly repaid, I will do my best to assist others when and where the opportunity appears.

You have noticed frequent reference to Emerson throughout this course. Every student of the course should own a copy of Emerson's Essays, and the essay on Compensation should be read and studied at least every three months. Observe, as you read this essay, that it deals with the same law as that upon which the Golden Rule is based.

There are people who believe that the Golden Rule philosophy is nothing more than a theory, and that it is in no way connected with an immutable law. They have arrived at this conclusion because of personal experience wherein they rendered service to others without enjoying the benefits of direct reciprocation.

How many are there who have not rendered service to others that was neither reciprocated nor appreciated? I am sure that I have had such an experience, not once, but many times, and I am equally sure that I will have similar experiences in the future, nor will I discontinue rendering service to others merely because *they* neither reciprocate nor appreciate my efforts.

And here is the reason:

When I render service to another, or indulge in an act of kindness, I store away in my sub-conscious mind the effect of my efforts, which may be likened to the 'charging' of an electric battery. By and by, if I indulge in a sufficient number of such acts I will have developed a positive, dynamic character that will *attract* to me people who harmonize with or resemble my own character.

Those whom I *attract* to me will reciprocate the acts of kindness and the service that I have rendered others, thus the Law of Compensation will have balanced the scales of justice for me, bringing back from one source the results of service that I rendered through an entirely different source.

You have often heard it said that a salesman's first sale should be to himself, which means that unless he first convinces himself of the merits of his wares, he will not be able to convince others. Here, again, enters this same Law of Attraction, for it is a well-known fact that *enthusiasm* is contagious, and when a salesman shows great *enthusiasm* over his wares, he will arouse a corresponding interest in the minds of others.

You can comprehend this law quite easily by regarding yourself as a sort of human magnet that attracts those whose characters harmonize with your own. In thus regarding yourself as a magnet that attracts to you all who harmonize with your dominating characteristics and repels all who do not so harmonize, you should keep in mind, also, the fact that *you are the builder of that magnet;* also, that you may change its nature so that it will correspond to any ideal that you may wish to set up and follow.

And, most important of all, you should keep in mind the fact that this entire process of change takes place through *thought!*

Your character is but the sum total of your *thoughts* and *deeds!* This truth has been stated in many different ways throughout this course.

Because of this great truth it is impossible for you to render any useful service or indulge in any act of kindness toward others without benefiting thereby. Moreover, it is just as impossible for you to indulge in any destructive *act* or *thought* without paying the penalty in the loss of a corresponding amount of your own power.

◆

Positive thought develops a dynamic personality. *Negative thought* develops a personality of an opposite nature. In many of the preceding lessons of this course, and in this one, definite instructions are given: as to the exact method of developing personality through *positive thought*. All of the formulas provided in this course are for the purpose of helping you *consciously* to direct the power of *thought* in the development of a personality that will attract to you those who will be of help in the attainment of your *definite chief aim*.

You need no proof that your hostile or unkind *acts* toward others bring back the effects of retaliation. Moreover, this retaliation is usually definite and immediate. Likewise, you need no proof that you can accomplish more by dealing with others in such a way that they will want to co-operate with you. If you mastered the eighth lesson, on self-control, you now understand how to induce others to act toward you as you wish them to act—*through your own attitude toward them.*

The law of 'an eye for an eye and a tooth for a tooth' is based upon the self-same law as that upon which the Golden Rule operates. This is nothing more than the law of retaliation with which all of us are familiar. Even the most selfish person will respond to this law, *because he cannot help it!* If I speak ill of you, even though I tell the truth, you will not think kindly of me. Furthermore, you will most likely retaliate in kind. But, if I speak of your virtues you will think kindly of me, and when the opportunity appears you will reciprocate in kind in the majority of instances.

Through the operation of this law of attraction the uninformed are constantly attracting trouble and grief and hatred and opposition from others by their *unguarded words* and *destructive acts.*

Do unto others as you would have them do unto you!

We have heard that injunction expressed thousands of times, yet how many of us understand the law upon which it is based? To make this injunction somewhat clearer it might be well to state it more in detail, about as follows:

Do unto others as you would have them do unto you, *bearing in mind the fact that human nature has a tendency to retaliate in kind.*

Confucius must have had in mind the law of retaliation when he stated the Golden Rule philosophy in about this way, 'Do not unto others that which you would not have them do unto you.'

And he might well have added an explanation to the effect that the reason for his injunction was based upon the common tendency of man to retaliate in kind.

Those who do not understand the law upon which the Golden Rule is based are inclined to argue that it will not work, for the reason that men are inclined toward the principle of exacting 'an eye for an eye and a tooth for a tooth', which is nothing more nor less than the law of retaliation. If they would go a step further in their reasoning, they would understand that they are looking at the *negative* effects of this law, and that the self-same law is capable of producing *positive* effects as well.

In other words, if you would not have your own eye plucked out, then insure against this misfortune by refraining from plucking out the other fellow's eye. Go a step further and render the other fellow an act of kindly, helpful service, and *through the operation of this same law of retaliation* he will render you a similar service.

And, if he should fail to reciprocate your kindness—what then?

You have profited, nevertheless, because of the effect of your act on *your own sub-conscious mind!*

Thus by indulging in acts of kindness and applying, always, the Golden Rule philosophy, you are sure of benefit from one source and at the same time you have a pretty fair chance of profiting from another source.

It might happen that you would base all of your acts toward others on the Golden Rule without enjoying any direct reciprocation for a long period of time, and it might so happen that those to whom you rendered those acts of kindness would never reciprocate, but meantime you have been adding vitality to your own character and sooner or later this *positive character* which you have been building will begin to assert itself and you will discover that you have been receiving compound interest on compound interest in return for those acts of kindness which appeared to have been wasted on those who neither appreciated nor reciprocated them.

Remember that your *reputation* is made by others, but your *character* is made by *you!*

You want your reputation to be a favourable one, but you cannot be sure that it will be for the reason that it is something that exists outside of your own control, in the minds of others. It is what others believe you to be. With your character it is different. Your character is that which *you are,* as the results of your *thoughts* and *deeds.* You control it. You can make it weak, good or bad. When you are satisfied and know in your mind that your character is above reproach you need not worry about your reputation, for it is as impossible for your character to be destroyed or damaged by anyone except yourself as it is to destroy matter or energy.

It was this truth that Emerson had in mind when he said, 'A political victory, a rise of rents, the recovery of your sick or the return of your absent friend, or some other quite external event raises your spirits, and you think your days are prepared for you. *Do not believe it.* It can never be so. *Nothing can bring you peace but yourself. Nothing can bring you peace but the triumph of principles.'*

One reason for being just toward others is the fact that such action may cause them to reciprocate, in kind, but a better reason is the fact that kindness and justice toward others develop *positive character* in all who indulge in these acts.

You may withhold from me the reward to which I am entitled for rendering you helpful service, but no one can deprive me of the benefit I will derive from the rendering of that service in so far as it adds to my own *character.*

GOLDEN RULE PHILOSOPHY

We are living in a great industrial age. Everywhere we see the evolutionary forces working great changes in the method and manner of living, and re-arranging the relationships between men, in the ordinary pursuit of life, liberty and a living.

This is an age of organized effort. On every hand we see evidence that organization is the basis of all financial success, and while other factors than that of organization enter into the attainment of success, this factor is still one of major importance.

This industrial age has created two comparatively new terms. One is called 'capital' and the other 'labour'. Capital and labour constitute the main wheels in the machinery of organized effort. These two great forces enjoy success in exact ratio to the extent that both understand and apply the Golden Rule philosophy. Despite this fact, however, harmony between these two forces does not always prevail, thanks to the destroyers of confidence who make a living by sowing the seed of dissension and stirring up strife between employers and employees.

During the past fifteen years I have devoted considerable time to the study of the causes of disagreement between employers and employees. Also, I have gathered much information on this subject from other men who, likewise, have been studying this problem.

There is but one solution which will, if understood by all concerned, bring harmony out of chaos and establish a perfect working relationship between capital and labour. The remedy is no invention of mine. It is based upon a great universal law of Nature. This remedy bas been well stated by one of the great men of this generation, in the following words,

'The question we propose to consider is exciting deep interest at the present time, but no more than its importance demands. It is one of the hopeful signs of the times that these subjects of vital interest to human happiness are constantly coming up for a bearing, are engaging the attention of the wisest men, and stirring the minds of all classes of people. The wide prevalence of this movement shows that a new life is beating in the heart of humanity, operating upon their faculties like the warm breath of spring upon the frozen ground and the dormant germs of the plant. It will make a great stir, it will break up many frozen and dead forms, it will produce great and, in some cases, it may be, destructive changes, but it announces the blossoming of new hopes, and the coming of new harvests for the supply of human wants and the means of greater happiness. There is great need of wisdom to guide the new forces coming into action. Every man is under the most solemn obligation to do his part in forming a correct public opinion and giving wise direction to popular will.

'The only solution for the problems of labour, of want, of abundance, of suffering and sorrow can only be found by regarding them from a moral and spiritual point of view. They must be seen end examined in a light that is not of themselves. *The true relations of labour and capital can never be discovered by human selfishness.* They must be viewed from a higher purpose than wages or the accumulation of wealth. They must be regarded from their bearing upon the purposes for which men was created. It is from this point of view I propose to consider the subject before us.

'Capital and labour are essential to each other. Their interests are so bound together that they cannot be separated. In civilized and enlightened communities, they are mutually dependent. If there is any difference, capital is more dependent upon labour than labour upon capital. Life can be sustained without capital. Animals, with a few exceptions, have no property, and take no anxious thought for the morrow, and our Lord commends them to our notice as examples worthy of imitation. "Behold the fowls of the air," He says, '"or they sow not, neither do they reap nor gather into barns, yet your heavenly Father feedeth them." The savages live without capital. Indeed, the great mass of human beings live by their labour from day to day, from hand to mouth. But no man can live upon his wealth. He cannot eat his gold and silver; he cannot clothe himself with deeds and certificates of stock. Capital can do nothing without labour, *and its only value consists in its power to purchase labour or its results*. It is itself the product of labour. It has no occasion, therefore, to assume an importance that does not belong to it. Absolutely dependent, however, as it is upon labour for its value, it is an essential factor in human progress.

'The moment man begins to rise from a savage and comparatively independent state to a civilized and dependent one, capital becomes necessary. Men come into more intimate relations with one another. Instead of each one doing everything, men begin to devote themselves to special employments, and to depend upon others to provide many things for them while they engage in some special occupation. In this way labour becomes diversified. One man works in iron, another in wood; one manufactures cloth, another makes it into garments; some raise food to feed those who build houses and manufacture implements of husbandry. This necessitates a system of exchanges, and to facilitate exchanges roads must be made, and men must be employed to make them. As population increases and necessities multiply, the business of exchange becomes enlarged, until we have immense manufactories, railroads girding the earth with iron bends, steamships ploughing every sea, and a multitude of men who cannot raise bread or make a garment, or do anything directly for the supply of their own wants.

'Now, we can see how we become more dependent upon others as our wants are multiplied and civilization advances. Each one works in his special employment, does better work, because he can devote his whole thought and time to a form of use for which he is specially fitted, and contributes more largely to the public good. While he is working for others, all others are working for him. Every member of the community is working for the whole body, and the whole body for every member. This is the law of perfect life, a law which rules everywhere in the material body. Every man who is engaged in any employment useful to body or mind is a philanthropist, a public benefactor, whether he raises corn on the prairie, cotton in Texas or India, mines coal in the chambers of the earth, or feeds it to engines in the hold of a steamship. If selfishness did not pervert and blast human motives, all men and women would be fulfilling the law of charity while engaged in their daily employment.

'To carry on this vast system of exchanges, to place the forest and the farm, the factory and the mine side by side, and deliver the products of all climes at every door, requires immense capital. One man cannot work his farm or factory, and build a railroad or a line of steamships. As raindrops acting singly cannot drive a mill or supply steam for an engine, but, collected in a vast reservoir, become the resistless power of Niagara, or the force which drives the engine and steamship like mighty shuttles from mountain to seacoast and from shore to shore, so a few dollars in a multitude of pockets are powerless to provide the means for these vast operations, but combined they move the world.

'Capital is a friend of labour and essential to its economical exercise and just reward. It can be, and often is, a terrible enemy, when employed for selfish purposes alone; but the great mass of it is more friendly to human happiness than is generally supposed. It cannot be employed without in some way, either directly or indirectly, helping the labourer. We think of the evils we suffer, but allow the good we enjoy to pass unnoticed. We think of the evils that larger means would relieve and the comforts they would provide, but overlook the blessings we enjoy that would have been impossible without large accumulations of capital. It is the part of wisdom to form a just estimate of the good we receive as well as the evils we suffer.

'It is a common saying at the present time, that the rich

are growing richer and the poor poorer; but when all man's possessions are taken into the account there are good reasons for doubting this assertion. It is true that the rich are growing richer. It is also true that the condition of the labourer is constantly improving. *The common labourer has conveniences and comforts which princes could not command a century ago.* He is better clothed, has a greater variety and abundance of food, lives in a more comfortable dwelling, and has many more conveniences for the conduct of domestic affairs and the prosecution of labour than money could purchase but a few years ago. An emperor could not travel with the ease, the comfort, and the swiftness that the common labourer can today. He may think that he stands alone, with no one to help. But, in truth, he has an immense retinue of servants constantly waiting upon him, ready and anxious to do his bidding. It requires a vast army of men and an immense outlay of capital to provide a common dinner, such as every man and woman, with few exceptions, has enjoyed today.

'Think of the vast combination of means and men and forces necessary to provide even a frugal meal. The Chinaman raises your tea, the Brazilian your coffee, the East Indian your spices, the Cuban your sugar, the farmer upon the western prairies your bread and possibly your beef, the gardener your vegetables, the dairyman your butter and milk; the miner has dug from the hills the coal with which your food was cooked and your house was warmed, the cabinet-maker has provided you with chairs and tables, the cutler with knives and forks, the potter with dishes, the Irishman has made your tablecloth, the butcher has dressed your meat, the miller your flour.

'But these various articles of food, and the means of preparing and serving them, were produced at immense distances from you and from one another. Oceans had to be traversed, hills levelled, valleys filled, and mountains tunnelled, ships must be built, railways constructed and a vast army of men instructed and employed in every mechanical art before the materials for your dinner could be prepared and served. There must also be men to collect these materials, to buy and sell and distribute them. Everyone stands in his own place and does his own work, and receives his wages. But he is none the less working for you, and serving you as truly and effectively as he would be if he were in your special employment and received his wages from your hand. In the light of these facts, which everyone must acknowledge, we may be able to see more clearly the truth, that every man and woman who does useful work is a public benefactor, and the thought of it and the purpose of it will ennoble the labour and the labourer. We are all bound together by common ties. The rich and the poor, the learned and the ignorant, the strong and the weak, are woven together in one social and civic web. Harm to one is harm to all; help to one is help to all.

'You see what a vast army of servants it requires to provide your dinner. Do you not see that it demands a corresponding amount of capital to provide and keep this complicated machinery in motion? And do you not see that every man, woman and child is enjoying the benefit of it? How could we get our coal, our meat, our flour, our tea and coffee, sugar and rice? The labourer cannot build ships and sail them and support himself while doing it. *The farmer cannot leave his farm and take his produce to the market. The miner cannot mine and transport his coal.* The farmer in Kansas may be burning corn today to cook his food and warm his dwelling, and the miner may be hungry for the bread which the corn would supply, because they cannot exchange the fruits of their labour. Every acre of land, every forest and mine has been increased in value by railways and steamboats, and the comforts of life and the means of social and intellectual culture have been carried to the most inaccessible places.

'But the benefits of capital are not limited to supplying present wants and comforts. It opens new avenues for labour. It diversifies it and gives a wider field to everyone to do the kind of work for which he is best fitted by natural taste and genius. The number of employments created by railways, steamships, telegraph and manufactories by machinery can hardly be estimated. Capital is also largely invested in supplying the means of intellectual and spiritual culture. Books are multiplied at constantly diminishing prices, and the best thought of the world, by means of our great publishing houses, is made accessible to the humblest workman. There is no better example of the benefits the common labourer derives from capital than the daily newspaper. For two or three cents the history of the world for twenty-four hours is brought to every door. The labourer, while riding to or from his work in a comfortable car, can visit all parts of the known world and get a truer idea of the events of the day than he could if he were bodily present. A battle in China or Africa, an earthquake in Spain, a dynamite explosion in London, a debate in Congress, the movements of men in public and private life for the suppression of vice, for enlightening the ignorant, helping the needy and improving the people generally, are spread before him in a small compass, and bring him into contact and on equality, in regard to the world's history, with kings and queens, with saints and sages and people in every condition in life. *Do you ever think,* while reading the morning paper, how many men have been running on your errands, collecting intelligence for you from all parts of the earth, and putting it into a form convenient for your use? It required the investment of millions and the employment of thousands of men to produce that paper and leave it at your door. And what did all this service cost you? A few cents.

'These are examples of the benefits which everyone derives from capital, benefits which could not be obtained without vast expenditures of money; benefits which come to us without our care and lay their blessings at our feet. Capital cannot be invested in any useful production without blessing a multitude of people. It sets the machinery of life in motion, it multiplies employment; it places the product of all climes at every door, it draws the people of all nations together; brings mind in contact with mind, and gives to every man and woman a large and valuable share of the product. These are facts which it would be well for everyone, however poor he may be, to consider.

'If capital is such a blessing to labour; if it can only be brought into use by labour, and derives all its value from it, how can there be any conflict between them? There could be none if both the capitalist and labourer acted from humane and Christian principles. But they do not. They are governed by inhuman and unchristian principles. Each party seeks to get the largest returns for the least service. Capital desires larger profits, labour higher wages. The interests of the capitalist and the labourer come into direct collision. In this warfare capital has great advantages, and has been prompt to take them. It has demanded and taken the lion's share of the profits. It has despised the servant that enriched it. It has regarded the labourer as a menial, a slave, whose rights and happiness it was not bound to respect. It influences legislators to enact laws in its favour, subsidizes governments and wields its power for its own advantage. Capital has been a lord and labour a servant. While the servant remained docile and obedient, content with such compensation as its lord chose to give, there was no conflict. But labour is rising from a servile, submissive and hopeless condition. It has acquired strength and intelligence; has gained the idea that it has rights that has rights that ought to be respected, and begins to assert and combine to support them.

'Each party in this warfare regards the subject from its own selfish interests. The capitalist supposes that gain to labour is loss to him, and that he must look to his own interests first; that the cheaper the labour the larger his gains. Consequently, it is for his interest to keep the price as low as possible. On the contrary, the labourer thinks that he loses what the capitalist gains, and, consequently, that it is for his interest to get as large wages as possible. From these opposite points of view their interests appear to be directly hostile. What one party gains the other loses; hence the conflict. Both are acting from selfish motives, and, consequently, must be wrong. Both parties see only half of the truth, and, mistaking that for the whole of it, they fall into a mistake ruinous to both. Each one stands on his own ground, and regards the subject wholly from his point of view and in the misleading light of his own selfishness. Passion inflames the mind and blinds the understanding; and when passion is aroused men will sacrifice their own interests to injure others, and both will suffer loss. They will wage continual warfare against each other; they will resort to all devices, and take advantage of every necessity to win a victory. Capital tries to starve the labourer into submission, like a beleaguered city; and hunger and want are most powerful weapons. Labour sullenly resists, and tries to destroy the value of capital by rendering it unproductive. If necessity or interest compels a truce, it is a sullen one, and maintained with the purpose of renewing hostilities as soon as there is any prospect of success. Thus, labourers and capitalists confront each other like two armed hosts, ready at any time to renew the conflict. *It will be renewed, without doubt, and continued with varying success until both parties discover that they are mistaken, that their interests are mutual, and can only be secured to the fullest extent by co-operation and giving to each the reward it deserves.* The capitalist and the labourer must clasp hands across the bottomless pit into which so much wealth and work has been cast.

'How this reconciliation is to be effected is a question that is occupying the minds of many wise and good men on both sides at the present time. Wise and impartial legislation will, no doubt, be an important agent in restraining blind passion and protecting all classes from insatiable greed; and it is the duty of every man to use his best endeavours to secure such legislation both in state and national governments. Organizations of laborers for protecting their own rights and securing a better reward for their labour, will have a great influence. That influence will continue to increase as their temper becomes normal and firm, and their demands are based *on justice and humanity.* Violence and threats will effect no good. Dynamite, whether in the form of explosives or the more destructive force of fierce and reckless passion, will heal no wounds nor subdue any hostile feeling. Arbitration is, doubtless, the wisest and most practicable means now available to bring about amicable relations between these hostile parties and secure justice to both. Giving the labourer a share in the profits of the business has worked well in some cases, but it is attended with great practical difficulties which require more wisdom, self-control and genuine regard for the common interests of both parties than often can be found. Many devices may have a partial and temporary effect. But no permanent progress can be made in settling this conflict without restraining and finally removing its cause.

'Its real central cause is an inordinate love of self and the world, and that cause will continue to operate as long as it exists. It may be restrained and moderated, but it will assert itself when occasion offers. Every wise man must, therefore, seek to remove the cause, and as far as he can do it he will control effects. Purify the fountain, and you make the whole stream pure and wholesome.

'There is a principle of universal influence that must underlie and guide every successful effort to bring these two great factors of human good which now confront each other with hostile purpose, into harmony. It is no invention or discovery of mine. It embodies a higher than human wisdom. It is not difficult to understand or apply. The child can comprehend it and act according to it. It is universal in its application, and wholly useful in its effects. It will lighten the burdens of labour and increase its rewards. It will give security to capital and make it more productive. It is simply the Golden Rule, embodied in these words, *'Therefore all things whatsoever ye would that men should do to you, do ye even so to them: for this is the law and the prophets.'*

'Before proceeding to apply this principle to the case in hand, let me call your special attention to it. It is a very remarkable law of human life which seems to have been generally overlooked by statesmen, philosophers and religious teachers. This rule embodies the whole of religion; it comprises all the precepts, commandments, and means of the future triumphs of good over evil, of truth over error, and the peace and happiness of men, foretold in the glorious visions of the prophets. Mark the words. It does not merely say that it is a wise rule; that it accords with the principles of the Divine order revealed in the law and the prophets. *It embodies them all; it "IS the law and the prophets."* It comprises love to God. It says we should regard Him as we desire to have Him regard us; that we should do to Him as we wish to have Him do to us. If we desire to have Him love us with all His heart, with all His soul, with all His mind, and with all His strength, we must love Him in the same manner. If we desire to have our neighbour love us as he loves himself, we must love him as we love ourself. Here, then, is the universal and Divine law of human service and fellowship. It is not a precept of human wisdom; it has its origin in the Divine nature, and its embodiment in human nature. Now, let us apply it to the conflict between labour and capital.

'You are a capitalist. Your money is invested in manufactures, in land, in mines, in merchandise, railways and ships, or you loan it to others on interest. You employ, directly or indirectly, men to use your capital. You cannot come to a just conclusion concerning your rights and duties and privileges by looking wholly at your own gains. The glitter of the silver and gold will exercise so potent a spell over your mind that it will blind you to everything else. You can see no interest but your own. The labourer is not known or regarded as a man who has any interests you are bound to regard. You see him only as your slave, your tool, your means of adding to your wealth. In this light he is a friend so far as he serves you, an enemy so far as he does not. But change your point of view. Put yourself in his place; put him in your place. How would you like to have him treat you if you were in his place? Perhaps you have been there. In all probability you have, for the capitalist today was the labourer yesterday, and the labourer today will be the employer tomorrow. You know from lively and painful experience how you would like to be treated. Would you like to be regarded as a mere tool? As a means of enriching another? Would you like to have your wages kept down to the bare necessities of life? Would you like to be regarded with indifference and treated with brutality? Would you like to have your blood, your strength, your soul coined into dollars for the benefit of another? These questions are easy to answer.

Everyone knows that he would rejoice to be treated kindly, to have his interests regarded, his rights recognized and protected. Everyone knows that such regard awakens a response in his own heart. Kindness begets kindness; respect awakens respect. Put yourself in his place. Imagine that you are dealing with yourself, and you will have no difficulty in deciding whether you should give the screw another turn, that you may wring a penny more from the muscles of the worker, or relax its pressure, and, if possible, add something to his wages, and give him respect for his service. Do to him as you would have him do to you in changed conditions.

'You are a labourer. You receive a certain sum for a day's work. Put yourself in the place of your employer. How would you like to have the men you employed work for you? Would you think it right that they should regard you as their enemy? Would you think it honest in them to slight their work, *to do as little and to get as much as possible?* If you had a large contract which must be completed at a fixed time or you would suffer great loss, would you like to have your workmen take advantage of your necessity to compel an increase of their wages? Would you think it right and wise in them to interfere with you in the management of your business? To dictate whom you should employ, and on what terms you should employ them? Would you not rather have them do honest work in a kind and good spirit? Would you not be much more disposed to look to their interests, to lighten their labour, to increase their wages when you could afford to do so, and look after the welfare of their families, when you found that they regarded yours? I know that it would be so. It is true that men are selfish, and that some men are so mean and contracted in spirit that they cannot see any interest but their own; whose hearts, not made of flesh but of silver and gold, are so hard that they are not touched by any human feeling, and care not how much others suffer if they can make a cent by it. But they are the exception, not the rule. We are influenced by the regard and devotion of others to our interests. The labourer who knows that his employer feels kindly toward him, desires to treat him justly and to regard his good, will do better work and more of it, and will be disposed to look to his employer's interests as well as his own.

'I am well aware that many will think this Divine and humane law of doing to others as we would have them do to us, is impracticable in this selfish and worldly age. If both parties would be governed by it, everyone can see how happy would be the results. But, it will be said, they will not. The labourer will not work unless compelled by want. He will take advantage of every necessity. As soon as he gains a little independence of his employer he becomes proud, arrogant and hostile. The employer will seize upon every means to keep the workmen dependent upon him, and to make as much out of them as possible. Every inch of ground which labour yields capital will occupy and intrench itself in it, and from its vantage bring the labourer into greater dependence and more abject submission. But this is a mistake. The history of the world testifies that when the minds of men are not embittered by intense hostility and their feelings outraged by cruel wrongs, they are ready to listen to calm, disinterested and judicious counsel. A man who employed a large number of laborers in mining coal told me that he had never known an instance to fail of a calm and candid response when he had appealed to honourable motives, as a man to man, both of whom acknowledged a common humanity. There is a recent and most notable instance in this city of the happy effect of calm, disinterested and judicious counsel in settling difficulties between employers and workmen that were disastrous to both.

'When the mind is inflamed by passion men will not listen to reason. They become blind to their own interests and regardless of the interests of others. *Difficulties are never settled while passion rages. They are never settled by conflict. One party may be subdued by power; but the sense of wrong will remain; the fire of passion will slumber ready to break out again on the first occasion.* But let the labourer or the capitalist feel assured that the other party has no wish to take any advantage, that there is a sincere desire and determination on both sides to be just and pay due regard to their common interests, and all the conflict between them would cease, as the wild waves of the ocean sink to calm when the winds are at rest. The labourer and the capitalist have a mutual and common interest. Neither can permanently prosper without the prosperity of the other. They are parts of one body. If labour is the arm, capital is the blood. Devitalize or waste the blood, and the arm loses its power. Destroy the arm, and the blood is useless. Let each care for the other, and both are benefited. *Let each take the Golden Rule as a guide,* and all cause of hostility will be removed, all conflict will cease, and they will go hand in hand to do their work and reap their just reward.'

POINTS TO REMEMBER

1. The Golden Rule means to do unto others as you would wish them to do unto you.
2. What you sow, you shall reap.
3. No man can attain success in its highest form without the aid of earnest prayer!

www.ingramcontent.com/pod-product-compliance
Lightning Source LLC
Chambersburg PA
CBHW032230080426
42735CB00008B/794